MEMORIES AND REPRESENTATIONS OF TERROR

Memories and Representations of Terror: Working Through Genocide explores how memories and representations shape our understanding of historical events, particularly the ways in which societies create narratives about genocide and its aftermath, using Argentina's last military dictatorship (1976–1983) and its contested legacy as a case study.

Feierstein examines how memories and representations of genocide are the terrain in which both the strategic objectives of genocide and the possibilities of challenging those objectives are contested. These memories and representations provide the foundation upon which critical judgments about the past are constructed and offer the potential for assuming responsibility and working through the consequences of genocide. This book proposes that terror continues to hijack the actions and identities of surviving societies via a process of the construction of memories and social representations of the lived experience in a final stage of genocide Feierstein terms "symbolic enactment." In doing so, Feierstein examines the contributions of various disciplines to comprehending memory processes and social representations. It covers a range of topics, from the nature of memory based on the neuroscientific discoveries of the last half-century to psychoanalytic theories on the functioning of the mind, including the role of psychic defense mechanisms, the unconscious mind, collective pacts of denial and different forms of desensitization. It also explores historiographical debates between forms of history and forms of memory, as well as sociological contributions to the analysis of social frames of memory, cultural memory, generational transmission and related issues.

The first volume of a three-volume work that aims to identify and evaluate the various consequences of genocidal social practices and the possibility of healing the scars left on individuals' subjectivities and the social fabric by genocide. This book is essential reading for students and academics in the humanities and social sciences with an interest in genocide, collective memory and identity.

Daniel Feierstein is Director of the Centre of Genocide Studies at the National University of Tres de Febrero, Argentina and Director of the Observatory of State Crimes at the University of Buenos Aires, Argentina. He is also a Senior Researcher at the National Research Council of Argentina (CONICET). His work primarily focuses on genocidal social practices and has been crucial in the increased recognition of the Argentine military junta's crimes as genocide. He is a previous President of the International Association of Genocide Scholars and has acted as a judge on the Permanent People's Tribunal in Sri Lanka, Mexico, Myanmar and Colombia. He is the author of several books, including *Genocide as a Social Practice: Reorganizing Society under the Nazis and Argentina's Military Juntas* (2014) and *Social and Political Representations of the COVID-19 Crisis* (Routledge, 2022). During the COVID-19 pandemic, Feierstein participated in numerous National and Provincial Advisory Councils in Argentina assessing the social aspects of the crisis.

Douglas Andrew Town is a British-born translator and writer. He lives in Buenos Aires, Argentina, where he directs the Master's program in Translation at the University of Belgrano. He has translated numerous books and articles from Spanish, German and French in various areas of the humanities and social sciences. He published his first novel, *Southern Waters*, in 2019.

MEMORIES AND REPRESENTATIONS OF TERROR

Working Through Genocide

Volume I

Daniel Feierstein

Translated by Douglas Andrew Town

LONDON AND NEW YORK

First published 2024
by Routledge
4 Park Square, Milton Park, Abingdon, Oxon OX14 4RN

and by Routledge
605 Third Avenue, New York, NY 10158

Routledge is an imprint of the Taylor & Francis Group, an informa business

© 2024 Daniel Feierstein

The right of Daniel Feierstein to be identified as author of this work has been asserted in accordance with sections 77 and 78 of the Copyright, Designs and Patents Act 1988.

All rights reserved. No part of this book may be reprinted or reproduced or utilised in any form or by any electronic, mechanical, or other means, now known or hereafter invented, including photocopying and recording, or in any information storage or retrieval system, without permission in writing from the publishers.

Trademark notice: Product or corporate names may be trademarks or registered trademarks, and are used only for identification and explanation without intent to infringe.

British Library Cataloguing-in-Publication Data
A catalogue record for this book is available from the British Library

ISBN: 978-1-032-37328-7 (hbk)
ISBN: 978-1-032-37326-3 (pbk)
ISBN: 978-1-003-33646-4 (ebk)

DOI: 10.4324/9781003336464

Typeset in Sabon
by KnowledgeWorks Global Ltd.

*To my Zeide Isaac, who taught me the first principles
of a thirst for justice with his laborious Spanish,
and whom, almost thirty years after his passing,
I still continue to need.
To Adriana Calvo, whose tireless drive to achieve
more, her perseverance and her candid and
critical voice in the face of our disagreements,
I still miss every day.*

CONTENTS

Acknowledgments		*viii*
	Introduction	1
1	Neuroscience and Memory Processes	10
2	Memory, Trauma and Working-Through	37
3	Memory Processes in the Social Sciences, History and Philosophy	62
4	How Concepts and Representations Shape Identity	87
5	The Symbolic Enactment of Genocide Through Representations in the Survivor Society	126
Index		*133*

ACKNOWLEDGMENTS

Over the years, I have met many people from whom I have learned countless academic, political or ethical lessons. The list has grown so long that there would not be enough space to include everybody, even if I tried. Here, I will mention some people, trusting that those not mentioned will understand that a process of inclusion and omission cannot always be fair or democratic. This is, after all, a book about the difficulties and subjectivity in constructing memory.

Here we go then.

On one level, this book owes a great deal to the friends and colleagues who participated in its conception and development. I want to thank the members of the Association of Former Detained and Disappeared of Argentina, the EATIP team (especially Lucila Edelman, Diana Kordon and Silvana Bekerman and also everyone who contributed to the discussion sessions of previous versions of the book), as well as dear researchers Malena Silveyra and Iván Fina (with whom I discuss these conceptual issues on a daily basis, and with whom I share personal and political connections), my sister Liliana Feierstein (whom I always bounce ideas off) and Beatriz Granda, and Alejandro Varela, who have helped me understand the complex connections between these topics and my own involvement.

I also wish to thank German social psychologist Christian Gudehus and his team at the Kulturwissenschaftfliches Institut in Essen, Germany, with whom I spent a research stay in early 2010 thanks to a scholarship from the Scholars in Residence program of the Goethe Institut to finish writing the Spanish version of this book. Thanks go, too, to the current team at the University of Bochum, with whom I have continued to collaborate for more than 10 years after my stay. We still organize meetings and debates on those topics relevant to the Spanish version of the book.

On an international level, I had the opportunity to discuss some of these ideas with Frank Chalk (from the Montreal Institute for Genocide and Human Rights Studies in Canada), Gabriel Gatti (from the University of the Basque Country in Bilbao), Penny Green and Thomas MacManus (from the State Crime Initiative at the Queen Mary University in the United Kingdom), Mofidul Hoque (from the Liberation War Museum in Dhaka, Bangladesh), Helen Jarvis (in Phnom Penh, Cambodia, who warmly welcomed me into her wooden cabin by the Mekong River), Alexander Laban Hinton, Nela Navarro and Doug Irvin-Erickson (from Rutgers University in the United States, where I taught several courses and gave lectures), Donna Lee Frieze (from Deakin University in Australia), Alberto Sucasas (from the University of La Coruña in Spain), Rafiki Ubaldo (from Rwanda, now in Sweden), Adam Müller and Andrew Woolford (from the University of Manitoba in Canada), and the United Nations Adviser on the Prevention of Genocide, Senegalese Adama Dieng, and his Spanish adviser, Mario Bull-Mercé, for the valuable discussions on genocide prevention that we had the opportunity to share in Siena, Oswiecim and Buenos Aires.

I am also grateful to Rodrigo Castro, Roberto Etchenique and Guillermo "Willy" Durán, for our debates on related topics within the Faculty of Exact and Natural Sciences at the University of Buenos Aires.

Likewise, I am indebted to Guillermo Levy, Hamurabi Noufouri, Adriana Taboada, Agustín Comotto, Gianni Tognoni (Secretary of the Permanent Peoples' Tribunal), members of my teams at the Center for Genocide Studies of the National University of Tres de Febrero (Eva Camelli, Natalia Crocco, Anita Jemio, Lucrecia Molinari, Bárbara Ohanian, Ludmila Schneider, Perla Sneh, Ely Stacco, Florencia Urosevich, Jorge Wozniak, Ana Zanotti, Lior Zylberman, and the always committed assistance of Claudia Massuh and Facundo Giménez). My thanks, too, to the Observatory of State Crimes of the University of Buenos Aires (which also includes many of the members of the CEG as well as María Belén Olmos, Pato Abalos Testoni Andrea Arce, Cecilia Bellia, Josefina Bergués, Aldana Campi, Laura Caponi, Augusto Carlucci, Walter Díaz, Agustina Fernández, Marcelo Ferreira, Matías Figal, Candela Gancedo, María Hereñú, Violeta Gimpelewicz, Romina Grilletta, Analía Martí, Lucía Massera, Denise Mayor Moreno, Ivana Ortiz, Macarena Peralta, María Pelle, Alan Rodríguez, Adrián Rojze, Sofía Sabaté, Cecilia Samanes, Catalina Seinhart, Alejandra y Julieta Stupenengo, Ana Laura Sucari, Ana Tauil, Gabriel Tchabrassian, Mariela Zelenay and Camila Zubcov), many of whom made sharp and suggestive contributions to improve this work or even to question central aspects of it and force me to refine and solidify my foundations.

Over the past 15 years, I have been invited to many interesting debates within the disciplines of psychiatry, psychology and psychoanalysis. I would especially like to highlight my conversations with Silvia Bentolila, Yago

Franco and Nicolás Vallejo as well as invitations from the Argentine Association of Psychology and Group Psychotherapy, the Argentine Psychoanalytical Association (APA) and the Psychoanalytic Association of Buenos Aires (Apdeba), among many others. I owe an enormous debt to each and every one of the human rights organizations in Argentina, but most especially to the survivors of the Argentine genocide for what they have taught me over a space of three decades.

On another level, I have benefited from specialist readers who have provided me with valuable criticisms and suggestions: Marcelo Burello and Rodrigo de Marco for Chapter 1; Eduardo Smalinsky and Ana Berezin for Chapter 2; Verónica Giménez Beliveau for Chapter 3. The contributions of Alejandro Alagia, Matías Bailone, Eduardo Barcesat, Osvaldo Barros, "Turca" Andrea Benites Dumont, Marga Cruz, Graciela Daleo, Eduardo Luis Duhalde, Cachito Fukman, Inés Izaguirre, Verónica Jeria, Carlos Loza, Rodolfo Mattarollo, Tina Meschiatti, Jorge Miranda, Horacio Ravenna, Carlos Rozanski, Carlos Slepoy, Raúl Eugenio Zaffaroni, among others, were fundamental in framing Chapter 4, whether these people agree or not with its assumptions.

I cannot fail to mention the broad institutional support I have received. This work is part of my research as a member of CONICET, an institution that I am honored to belong to and that has always supported my projects. In turn, my position as a researcher has always been at the National University of Tres de Febrero, whose authorities (Rector, Vice-Rector, Academic Secretary) have consistently supported and assisted each and every one of my projects. Likewise, the course I have been teaching since 2001 as a special sociology professor at the University of Buenos Aires ("Analysis of genocidal social practices") and the Open Seminar in 2016 ("The system of concentration camps in Argentina") have proved highly enriching. I have benefited from the contributions of hundreds of eloquent, committed and critical students from whom I have undoubtedly learned as much or more than they have learned from me. I also want to thank FCE, and especially Alejandro Archaín and Mariana Rey, for having trusted in this work when it was just a mere outline.

Finally, there is the militant contribution of hundreds and thousands of comrades who have fought and continue to fight for a better Argentina and a better world, and who are always present in these pages. I am proud to have traveled side by side with some of them, such as Justicia Ya, Liga Argentina por los Derechos Humanos, Comisión por la Memoria, la Verdad y la Justicia de Zona Norte, the different regionals of the Asamblea Permanente por los Derechos Humanos, the different regional branches of HIJOS, the Instituto Espacio por la Memoria, the Archivo Nacional de la Memoria, the Comisión Provincial por la Memoria, the Tribunal Permanente de los Pueblos, the International Association of Genocide Scholars.

Turning now to the English version of this book, I would like to thank Rebecca Brennan and Chris Parry for their interest in publishing it with Routledge and also Chris Parry for his help with editing. To Barbara Rattner for her confidence in this work and for suggesting its possible destination. I would like to say a special word of thanks to Douglas Andrew Town, who was not only an exquisite translator but also a coauthor of this English version, adding numerous comments, suggestions and corrections that have undoubtedly enriched it. A special thanks to Luigi Zoja, an Italian psychoanalyst and scholar who enriched very much my views on different subjects analyzed in this book. Finally, I wish to thank the reviewers of this book, for their valuable comments that improved and enriched this version.

My parents, Tito and Susana, and my sister Liliana have always been my point of origin, and part of those social frameworks that constitute who we can become.

My children, Ezequiel and Tamara, continue to be the affective foundation without which nothing presented here would be possible, as well as the possibility of vital (but also moral) persistence in the world. Certainly, I have made more mistakes with them than the average father, but lack of love will never be one of them. Their love, on the other hand, has always been and continues to be a light that shines brightly in moments of pain, danger or skepticism.

To my partner, Virginia Feinmann, in whom I found not only the depths of love and desire but also the possibility of discovering (and narrating to myself) unknown parts of myself and also, why not, of discovering another version of me.

INTRODUCTION

This is the first of a three-volume work that sets out to identify and evaluate the different consequences of genocidal social practices and the possibility to work through them. As such, it shares the theoretical and political concerns of my previous books, in particular *Genocide as Social Practice* (Feierstein, 2014) and *Seis estudios sobre Genocidio* (*Six Studies on Genocide*) (Feierstein, 1997, 2000). However, it is more wide-ranging than these earlier works – especially with its incursions into neuroscience, psychoanalysis and criminal law.

All three volumes of the present series – *I: Memories and Representations, II: Judgments* and *III: Responsibilities* – seek to work through the scars left on individuals' subjectivities and on the social fabric by genocidal social practices. This first volume focuses on memories and representations of massive State Crimes, with a final case study focusing on the Argentina's last military dictatorship (1976–1983). Although important in its own right, here this example has been chosen primarily to allow for reflection on broader issues. The second volume deals with the problem of judgment. Judgment is used both in a philosophical sense (our ability to judge as part of the mechanisms of consciousness) and to refer to criminal proceedings against those responsible for genocidal social practices. Again, the case study focuses on Argentina but the intention is to transcend the idiosyncrasies of those hearings in order to understand the role of the judiciary (either at an international, regional or national level) regarding the human capacity of judgment. The third volume is devoted to a critical analysis of different levels of responsibility for genocide.

This is a rapidly growing area of research on memories and representations and one that clearly needs to move beyond the fixed taxonomies and

DOI: 10.4324/9781003336464-1

rigid understandings of reality that still characterizes many disciplines. Neuroscience, psychoanalysis, philosophy, the social sciences and the arts have all produced competing theories of memory and memory representation. Yet there has been little cross-fertilization among them. In the few cases where collaboration has been attempted, the results have generally proved unsatisfactory, despite the fact that most memory researchers – often unwittingly – address very similar hypotheses.

The neurosciences have mostly been concerned with trying to find the material substrate of memory (its physical location in the brain), and with explaining and endeavoring to treat certain memory disorders. However, unless we understand why the human psyche exists in the first place, as well as the importance of social interactions for creating and maintaining it, it is impossible to understand memory, let alone memory representations or something even more complex like social or collective representations, which are not placed in any part of a non-existent "collective brain."

Sigmund Freud's original work, with its broad interdisciplinary sweep, seemed to offer just such an understanding. Later generations of psychoanalysts, however, have tended to ignore the biochemical substrate on which our psychic apparatus is based, so downplaying the role of physical causes in mental illness. Worse still, they have refused to examine the socio-political and philosophical implications of their own psychoanalytical theories. Consequently, psychoanalysis has increasingly separated the psychic apparatus from the material and social elements that organize and structure it, either from the biological elements and also from the social ones. Some psychoanalysts still propose outdated explanations for the split between body and consciousness, such as the mind-body distinction made by Descartes at a time when neuroscience, psychoanalysis and social science did not even exist (Descartes, 1984 [1641]).

On the other hand, the social sciences have become bogged down during the last half century in Byzantine arguments over the kind of possible relations between history and memory. As a result, they have generally ignored developments in other disciplines such as neuroscience and psychoanalysis, including developments that show many of their own ideas to be either irrelevant or even demonstrably false. Unfortunately, there is no room in a volume of this length to consider the peculiarly rich and complex relationship of aesthetics and art with memory and how it could enrich the different analysis developed in this volume (a debt for a new volume).

Of course, this does not mean there have been no attempts to cross-disciplinary boundaries. As mentioned earlier, Freud himself favored an interdisciplinary approach, for example in his forgotten *Psychology for Neurologists* (which his translator Strachey called *A Scientific Project*). Many of his reflections in *Beyond the Pleasure Principle*; *Totem and Taboo*; or *Moses and Monotheism* are in a similar vein. These are just a few of his works that seek to establish a dialogue between psychoanalysis and neurology in the first and second case, or psychoanalysis and the social sciences in the rest of them (Freud, 1955a, 1955b, 1964, 1966).

Also worth mentioning are Jean-Pierre Changeux and Paul Ricœur's attempts to create an exchange of ideas between neurology and philosophy, despite Ricœur's difficulties with a language he feels uncomfortable with and is obviously unwilling to master (Changeux & Ricoeur, 2000). Then there is genetic psychology and, in particular, the brilliant transdisciplinary intuitions of Jean Piaget and his disciple Rolando García in works such as *The Equilibration of Cognitive Structures, Psychogenesis and the History of Science* and *Sistemas Complejos (Complex Systems)*, among many other works (García, 2006; Piaget, 1977, 1985; Piaget & García, 1989).

Finally, neuroscientists such as Edelman (1989, 1990, 1992, 2004, 2006; Edelman & Tononi, 2000), Kandel (2007) and Rosenfield (1992, 1988) have tried to open up neurology to other disciplines through their occasional but important contributions to sociology and psychology. All these attempts, however, have been the exception rather than the rule.

Having said this, I should make it clear that I have no overarching knowledge of the disciplines I have just mentioned, nor do I set out to explore all the possible interconnections among them. The aim is not to give a state-of-the-art account of the work in each field, but to understand how memory processes affect personal and social identities. Accordingly, I will examine only those that clarify and support the hypotheses that guide this trilogy, especially those presented in this first book. My main focus will be the social sciences, given that they are my own area of expertise. However, when incorporating contributions from other fields, I will try to respect each discipline's logic and way of constructing knowledge at that particular level of analysis.

This first volume explores the ideas of a selected group of authors from the neurosciences already mentioned (Gerald Edelman, Eric Kandel, Jean-Pierre Changeux and Israel Rosenfield); psychoanalysis (mostly Sigmund Freud, but also studies of trauma by Käes (1976, 2007), Puget and Kaës (1991), and the members of the Argentine Team for Psychosocial Work and Research [EATIP; Kordon et al., 2012], among others); philosophy (Benjamin, 1969; Bergson, 1944; Ricœur, 2004, among others) and sociology, social psychology and history (including Assmann 2006; Bartlett, 1932; Halbwachs, 1992; LaCapra, 1998, among others). Most of the work examined is on the trauma generated by genocide in the sense of social practices aimed at destroying and reorganizing the relationships within a society (Feierstein, 2014).

The book is organized as follows:

Chapter 1 introduces neuroscience and some of the fundamental findings of the last 40 years with regard to brain functioning. These findings will be used to suggest hypotheses about the adaptive nature of what I will call "desensitization processes," as well as to highlight the creative and *non-reproductive* nature of human memory. As Gerard Edelman points out, "[memory] is in some sense a form of constructive recategorization during ongoing experience, rather than a precise replication of a previous sequence of events" (Edelman & Tononi, 2000, p. 95).

Chapter 2 develops some basic concepts from Freud's work and explains how they related to the ideas in the previous chapter. It then returns to the notion of desensitization, which it illuminates with René Käes and Janine Puget's psycho-sociological concept of "denegative pacts," (Käes, 1976, 2007; Puget & Käes, 1991, 2007) that is, an unconscious agreement not to mention the traumatic event. These ways of representing the reality – as something nonsensical, irrational, even inexpressible – loom large in the discourses of horror and I refer to them here as "ideologies of non-meaning." My thesis is that such discourses – sometimes intentionally – prevent the survivors of genocide coming to terms with traumatic terror.

Chapter 3 approaches these hypotheses – desensitization, denegative pacts and the effects of non-meaning – from various philosophical, historical and the social science perspectives. Specifically, it examines the link between memory and action (Bergson), and memory and identity (Ricœur) in order to show how the static nature of "irrational" or "ineffable" memories makes it almost impossible for sufferers to own and come to terms with their trauma. Similarly, this third chapter uses some of Walter Benjamin's critical intuitions to reformulate the sterile discussion on the differences between memory and history, and to emphasize the socio-political character of both.

Chapter 4 applies the concepts developed in the previous chapters to critically evaluate different ways of representing and describing massive state violence, such as war, genocide, state terrorism, crimes against humanity in the different collective reconstructions and social memories. It seeks to break the existing deadlock over definitions and bring these in line with reality, based on empirical evidence. It points out that war, genocide, State terrorism and crimes against humanity are highly abstract concepts. The real question is not where each definition begins and ends, but the different ways the *narratives* created by these concepts transform identities, whether personal, group or collective. This analysis incorporates the notions of desensitization, denegative pacts and forms of appropriation of or alienation from personal experience. It also includes the types of relationship established between past and present and the role played by the ideologies of non-meaning in making experience irrational and unrepresentative.

The purpose of the first three chapters, then, is to pave the way for Chapter 4, which discusses the intersubjective and socio-political consequences of different ways of defining and narrating massive state violence. The empirical support for these ideas comes from studies of State violence and trauma in Argentina, but the approach and conceptual tools presented here are obviously relevant to comprehending other historical events that may have been characterized very differently.

Chapter 5 adds a kind of coda regarding my concept of symbolical enactment of genocide developed in previous works (Feierstein, 2000, 2014) and its connection with the analysis of representations developed in previous chapters.

I should point out that my approach is not neutral. That would hardly be possible. On the contrary, although the scope of this book is wider, one of its aims is to provide a more solid foundation for the use of the term "genocide" to characterize the massive state violence that occurred in Argentina in the 1970s. As we will see, genocide, with its multiple legal and symbolic implications, provided the best narrative for overcoming trauma and illuminating those aspects of the historical process that remained invisible in other narratives. So, it is not a question that genocide is "the most serious crime" or the most horrible one. It has nothing to do with levels of horror. On the contrary, one of the objectives of this volume is to highlight the importance of the genocide concept in the construction of a narrative of the past which could help in the working through the trauma.

Nevertheless, this in no way implies that the concept of genocide is applicable to every historical situation or it is a kind of conceptual recipe to help the healing process. Nor does it mean that examples cannot be found – as will be seen briefly in the case of Guatemala – in which narratives constructed around the concept of genocide have done more harm than good. Indeed, in the case of Guatemala, the emphasis on ethnicity has made it more difficult to take responsibility for and process the events in question, both theoretically and politically. In short, the debate is not only or even fundamentally about which theoretical concepts to use but about the type of narrative each concept implies in any historical case and the different consequences of each of those narratives.

As mentioned before, unlike my previous legal or historical works, many of which have been cited in court sentences, this book aims to go deeper. It examines the ultimate theoretical and political justification for applying the concept of genocide to recent events in Argentine history (taking genocide here to mean a "partial destruction of the Argentine national group" as the most important meaning) and how this concept shapes a specific narrative. In other words, this book no longer seeks to prove that genocide took place in Argentina as was the case in many previous works and in numerous court proceedings. Rather, it shows the advantages for memory and healing that come from representing these events in Argentina as genocide rather than as war, state terrorism or crimes against humanity.

Fortunately, Argentine society has been characterized by a strong resistance to denialist or minimizing approaches, although these have reappeared since 2013. The widespread repudiation among the population of Argentina's last dictatorship has been fundamental in bringing to trial and convicting those responsible for massive human rights violations. Unlike many other countries, prosecutions currently have no statute of limitations or other restrictions. Trials are held in national courts (not international bodies or special chambers), and the rights of the accused are scrupulously protected even though these were the worst crimes committed in Argentina in the last century. Few societies can boast as much.

The exceptional nature of these prosecutions, the number of cases on trial and – most importantly – the participation of different sectors of civil society has given rise to deep and complex debates on memory and healing. These constitute the background to this three-volume work and prevent us becoming sidetracked with more conventional discussions of "transitional" processes. Questions about whether impunity laws are admissible, or forgiveness and reconciliation are possible without justice, seem to have been resolved in Argentina, and are no longer a subject of debate.

The complex relationship between our human capacity for judgment and real-life judgments, on the one hand, and preexisting processes of memories and representations of lived experiences, on the other, are addressed in the second volume of this work entitled *Judgments*. Suffice it to say for the time being that since the end of the last military dictatorship, Argentine society has managed – with occasional setbacks – to begin one of the most complex and profound discussions on how populations can cope with the effects of the massive state destruction of groups of their members. To what extent can certain forms of memory and representation either perpetuate the terror or contribute to the healing process. Again, at the risk of sounding reiterative, simply labeling such processes as genocide solves very little. The processes are far too complex. Rather we need to understand the healing potential of the narratives it creates.

In this sense, another aim of this first volume is to contribute to the ongoing debate in Argentine society on the reciprocal relationship between collective memory and lawmaking and law enforcement. This is currently a hot topic in many Argentine courthouses, social movements, universities, neighborhood associations, labor unions and student organizations, political parties and in all human rights organizations.

I am fully aware that this trilogy, as well as my previous work, may be on the wrong track. This can also be said of the work of many social, political and human rights groups with whom I have shared these debates and the struggle for justice over the past 40 years. Only time will tell if my approach is the correct one, and what the next steps should be. In any case, I would like to make it clear that I deeply respect those colleagues or organizations – whether Argentinean or otherwise – who do not share my views on the importance of the term "genocide" to describe the Argentine and other cases and consider concepts such as crimes against humanity, State terrorism or civil war to be more suitable, useful or powerful.

Whatever your position on these matters, I assure you that this book not only reflects my deepest personal conviction, but is the result of many years of careful reading, study and reflection. I have considered the social implications of each of the narratives presented here with the greatest care and responsibility. Of course, I will welcome any comments that help clarify the problems of applying a genocide narrative to the Argentine case (some of which are analyzed in this book). I also hope that those colleagues, academics, lawyers and activists who disagree with my views will join the debate and explain why they consider other types of historical narrative are preferable.

I would like to end this introduction with a short anecdote. In 2006, Federal Oral Tribunal No. 1 of La Plata – made up of judges Carlos Rozanski, Norberto Lorenzo and Horacio Isaurralde – became the first Argentine court to recognize that genocide had taken place in Argentina. Since then more than 40 other courts have done so, including those of the provinces of Santiago del Estero, Tucumán and Mendoza or the city of Mar del Plata, among many others. The first person to be sentenced for genocide was the deputy chief of police of the Province of Buenos Aires, Miguel Osvaldo Etchecolatz. Similar sentences were handed down by the same court in the cases of the priest Christian Von Wernich and the staff who worked in Penitentiary Unit No. 9 of La Plata. The reading of the sentence at the 2006 trial was filmed by numerous organizations. There is a very good edition by the Buenos Aires Province Commission for Memory (CPM) that I especially recommend.

Please notice the expressions of peace, satisfaction and joy on the faces of the survivors and the victims' relatives as the judges read out the words "crimes committed in the context of genocide." These faces tell – on an emotional level – of the healing potential of certain "legal truths." This first volume attempts to explain the *how* and *why* of this healing potential maybe in a kind of theoretical terms.

References

Assmann, J. (2006). *Religion and cultural memory: Ten studies* (R. Livingstone, Trans.). Stanford University Press.

Bartlett, F. C. (1932). *Remembering: A study in experimental and social psychology.* Cambridge University Press.

Benjamin, W. (1969). *Illuminations* (H. Zohn, Trans., with an introduction by Hannah Arendt, Eds.). Schocken Books.

Bergson, H. (1944) [1911]. *Creative evolution* (A. Mitchell, authorized Trans.). The Modern Library.

Changeux, J. P. (2009). *The physiology of truth. Neuroscience and human knowledge.* Harvard University Press.

Changeux, J. P. (2012). *The good, the true, and the beautiful: A neuronal approach* (G. Laurence, Trans.). Yale University Press.

Changeux, J. P., & Ricoeur, P. (2000). *What makes us think? A neuroscientist and a philosopher argues about ethics, human nature and the brain* (M. B. DeBevoise, Trans.). Princeton University Press. https://doi.org/10.1515/9780691238265

Descartes, R. (1984) [1641]. Meditations on first philosophy. In J. Cottingham, R. Stoothoff, & D. Murdoch (Trans.), *The philosophical writings of René Descartes* (Vol. 2, pp. 1–62). Cambridge University Press.

Edelman, G. M. (1989). *The remembered present*. Basic Books.

Edelman, G. M. (1990). *Neural Darwinism*. Oxford Paperbacks.

Edelman, G. M. (1992). *Bright air, brilliant fire*. Basic Books.

Edelman, G. M. (2004). *Wider than the sky: The phenomenal gift of consciousness*. Yale University Press.

Edelman, G. M. (2006). *Second nature: Brain science and human knowledge*. Yale University Press.

Edelman, G. M., & Tononi, G. (2000). *A universe of consciousness: How matter becomes imagination*. Basic Books.

Feierstein, D. (1997). *Cinco estudios sobre genocidio*. Acervo Cultural.

Feierstein, D. (2000). *Seis estudios sobre genocidio. Análisis de las relaciones sociales: otredad, exclusion, exterminio*. EUDEBA.

Feierstein, D. (2014). *Genocide as social practice. Reorganizing society under Nazism and Argentina´s military juntas*. Rutgers University Press. (Spanish original version: *El genocidio como práctica social: entre el nazismo y la experiencia argentina*, Buenos Aires, FCE, 2007).

Freud, S. (1955a) [1913–1914]. Totem and taboo and other works. In J. Strachey, & A. Freud (Eds.), *The standard edition of the complete psychological works of Sigmund Freud* (Vol. XIII). The Hogarth Press and the Institute of Psycho-Analisis. ix–164

Freud, S. (1955b) [1920]. Beyond the pleasure principle. In J. Strachey, & A. Freud (Eds.), *The standard edition of the complete psychological works of Sigmund Freud* (Vol. XVIII). The Hogarth Press and the Institute of Psycho-Analisis.

Freud, S. (1964) [1937–1939]. Moses and monotheism. In Strachey, J. & A. Freud (eds.), *The standard edition of the complete psychological works of Sigmund Freud* (Vol. XXIV). The Hogarth Press and the Institute of Psycho-Analisis. 3–140.

Freud, S. (1966) [1895]. A project for a scientific psychology. In J. Strachey, & A. Freud (Eds.), *The standard edition of the complete psychological works of Sigmund Freud* (Vol. I). The Hogarth Press and the Institute of Psycho-Analisis. 283–413.

García, R. (2006). *Sistemas complejos. Conceptos, método y fundamentación epistemológica de la investigación interdisciplinaria*. Gedisa.

Halbwachs, M. (1992). *On collective memory* (Lewis A. Coser, Ed. & Trans. with an Introduction). University of Chicago Press.

Käes, R. (1976). *L´Appareil psychique groupal. Constructions du groupe*. Bordas Dunod.

Käes, R. (2007). *Un singulier pluriel. La psychanalisé á l´épreuve du groupe*. Dunod.

Kandel, E. R. (2007). *In search of memory: The emergence of a new science of mind*. W. W. Norton & Company.

Kordon, D., Edelman, E., Lagos, D., & Kersner, D. (2012). *South, dictatorship and after: Psychosocial and clinical elaboration of collective traumas*. EATIP Argentine

Team of Psychosocial Work and Research. http://www.eatip.org.ar/wp-content/uploads/2012/06/South-dictatorship-and-after...-Psychosocial-and-clinical-elaboration-of-collective-traumas.pdf

LaCapra, D. (1998). *History and memory after Auschwitz*. Cornell University Press.

Piaget, P. (1977). *The grasp of consciousness: Action and concept in the young child*. Routledge.

Piaget, P. (1985). *The equilibration of cognitive structures: The Central problem of intellectual development*. University of Chicago Press.

Piaget, P., & García, R. (1989). *Psychogenesis and the history of science*. Columbia University Press.

Puget, J., & Kaës, R. (Eds.) (1991). *Violencia de Estado y psicoanálisis*. Lumen.

Ricoeur, P. (2004). *Memory, history, forgetting* (K. Blamey, & D. Pellauer, Trans.). University of Chicago Press.

Rosenfield, I. (1988). *The invention of memory: A new view of the brain*. Basic Books.

Rosenfield, I. (1992). *The strange, familiar and forgotten*. Alfred Knopf.

1
NEUROSCIENCE AND MEMORY PROCESSES

In the second half of the 19th century, work on brain-damaged patients suggested that certain regions of the brain were responsible for certain functions. In attempting to identify these functions, however, neurologists soon came up against the tremendous complexity of brain functioning and the integration of different areas of the brain in even the simplest processes. In 1962, biologist Francis Schmitt coined the term neuroscience to refer to a new interdisciplinary science focusing on the structure and functioning of the nervous system, but it was not until 1990 that Seiji Ogawa's functional magnetic resonance imaging (fMRI) made it possible to measure brain's activity based on blood flow. More recently, the development of neuroimaging and other powerful measurement techniques has allowed neuroscientists to observe how nerve cells behave when connected together to form neural pathways, neural circuits and larger brain networks, and to hypothesize about how cognition and emotion are mapped to specific neural substrates.

Nevertheless, the discoveries of neuroscience – although fascinating – explain only a small part of the way our brains function. As Hilary and Steven Rose point out in their scientific and political critique of the "neuro" disciplines, such an approach "assumes our brains are somehow separate from our embodied location in the complex intersections of the cultural, social, economic, historic and environmental" (Rose & Rose, 2016, p. 88). More generally, neuroscience has underpinned various clandestine projects to develop brainwashing techniques, something which is still significant today (Rose, 2006).[1]

Although Karl Lashley discovered in 1950 that memories are not localized but distributed across the brain (Lashley, 1950), in the decades that followed few memory researchers focused on memory processes – in other words,

DOI: 10.4324/9781003336464-2

the processes by which the brain encodes, stores and later recalls information. Those who did, such as Eric Kandel (2007), Gerald Edelman (1989, 1990, 2002, 2004, 2006) and Edelman and Tononi (2000), or Jean-Pierre Changeux (2009, 2012), among others, soon realized although specific brain regions are responsible for particular cognitive functions, even elementary memory operations depend on large numbers of these regions to produce what social scientists call memory. At the same time, they were quick to realize the enormous plasticity of the nervous system, especially the brain. This plasticity explains how individual differences in brain structure and functioning are the result of individual development.

Rather than examining the architecture or structure of the memory system, then, or the effects of brain damage on cognitive performance, this first volume will explore the *processes* operating within the system. This approach is consistent with the current consensus in neuroscience that memories are not "recorded" in the brain, but are reconstructed from multiple systems – olfactory, visual, gustatory, semantic, episodic and procedural, among many others. The number of these systems is unclear as researchers continue to discover new ones. What is clear, however, is that it is the *interaction* among these systems that gives rise to what we think of as memory.

To summarize what has been said so far, memories are *not* recorded like audio or video tapes but are *constructed*. They are the *creative* result of complex and diverse processes in the neural substrate (the central nervous system) but they are not themselves located in any specific area of the brain.

This chapter is based mainly on the research of Gerald Edelman,[2] Eric Kandel[3] and Jean-Pierre Changeux.[4] Gerald Edelman's research preceded, accompanied and continued that of Giulio Tononi and Israel Rosenfield, among others, and has been popularized by writers such as Oliver Sacks (1997, 2005) and Jonah Lehrer (2007). The works of these neuroscientists may prove linguistically difficult, epistemologically questionable or politically provocative for some readers. However, we will see that they share numerous assumptions with other disciplinary fields and add to, rather than subtract from, the message of the book. The challenge is to respect the logic of each level of explanation.

Why start with the neurosciences? A quick guide to this chapter

To prevent any misunderstandings right from the start, I would like to repeat that my aim is not to provide a complete neuroscientific account of memory or identity processes. This has already been attempted by some neuroscientists. As mentioned in the introduction, this volume sets out to analyze the importance of memory and representation for identity. More precisely, it is concerned with the disruption and transformation of memories and representations caused by the systematic annihilation of population groups as part of a technology of power designed to reorganize society. This is a topic I have developed in previous works from the point of view of history, sociology and law (Feierstein, 2000, 2014). In this volume, however, I recognize the need for a much more specific understanding of terror and of how social relations are reorganized differently by different memory representations. I also propose ways of working through the effects of terror in order to reverse the social engineering carried out by the perpetrators of mass state violence – or at least facilitate healthier forms of social relations.

Our efforts to understand the effects of terror have often been hampered by a lack of interdisciplinary dialogue. This problem, in turn, has led to speculation about how memory works based entirely on assumptions about the *purpose* of terror. Naturally, this chapter will not solve these problems once and for all. What it can do, is to take the discoveries in neuroscience – some consolidated, others less so – and use them to illuminate a different set of ideas. Care must be taken, however, not to confuse different levels of explanation or to fall into reductionism. Lack of dialogue between disciplines, for example, has led some neuroscientists to develop analogies between the behavior of neural networks and higher level psychological, behavioral, sociological and even philosophical and ethical phenomena.[5] In doing so, they have simply fallen into banal attempts to justify their own pre-scientific prejudices with supposedly scientific explanations.

On the other hand, it is also true that the social sciences and psychoanalysis have tended to analyze social relations and the human psyche as if they were disembodied abstractions inscribed on thin air. In this way, they have reinforced the Cartesian notion of mind-body separation, and even the idea of a definitive split between "man" and the animal kingdom. In the same way, various phenomenological studies have also been conducted. Linton, for example, used largely introspective methods to develop a hierarchy of autobiographical memory, with interlocking structures of time periods and themes (Linton, 1975, 1986). In many cases, however, these disciplines have reached conclusions that are totally unsustainable in the light of current knowledge of physiology and brain functioning.

The purpose of this chapter, then, is ambitious and no doubt problematic. Respecting the logic of each discipline, it aims to show how hypotheses generated at the biological level could be tested at other levels to shed light on memory, representation and identity. It is up to the reader to judge to what extent this goal has been achieved.

The brain as an adaptive organ

One of the most thought-provoking aspects of much neuroscientific work is its evolutionary approach to brain function. Gerald Edelman, for example, argues that human cognition is adaptive. As it engages with reality, the brain develops more effective responses and inhibits those which have failed. This approach differs radically from that of many neuroscientists and philosophers who have tried to model human cognition on artificial intelligence (AI) or cybernetics. Edelman shows that the brain does *not* process data sequentially (i.e. step-by-step) like a conventional computer. On the contrary, brain function is permanently evolving and changing.

For Edelman, memory and consciousness are processes, not things or properties. Memory and consciousness do not exist as such, but are products of a continual and uninterrupted process of construction thanks to the amazing plasticity of brain functioning (Ansermet & Magistretti, 2004). This idea is crucial to our understanding of the problems discussed later in this book. It differs radically from the earlier assumptions of many neuroscientists and philosophers who used digital computer as a model of cognition, and attempted to draw parallels between thinking and "artificial intelligence." An example of this computer-based approach is found in the work of Adam Zeman (2003, 2006).

Now, the notion of the brain as an organ shaped by processes of natural selection is not only plausible. It is strongly in line with the work of Sigmund Freud and Jean Piaget (Piaget, 1977, 1985; Piaget & García, 1989), who anticipated many of the findings of neuroscience by several decades. Unfortunately, in the case of Freud, these intuitions were lost as the dialogue between neurologists and psychoanalysts dried up. In fact, evolutionary theory has been under attack in some quarters for nearly a century – particularly for the way Darwin's theory has been used in pseudoscientific ways to justify genocide and racism. In the 21st century, it is difficult to find a social science approach in the Spanish-speaking world centered on what biologists call "natural selectionism," while Edelman's term "Neural Darwinism" would frighten even legal researchers.

On the other hand, without an understanding of how the brain functions, many historical-sociological theories about memory processes are forced to assume Cartesian dualism – a sharp separation between conscious processes and their physical substrate. This limitation condemns would-be researchers to speculative methods. And once the "human mind" becomes divorced from its physiological basis in the body, the most diverse forms of idealism can arise without any connection to "reality" in the philosophical sense.

This is not to say that Cartesian dualism has not proved productive in the past. Until the late 19th century, it was a way of freeing philosophy, psychology and social sciences from a biology that was technically and epistemologically incapable of explaining the physical basis of consciousness and memory. Thanks to this freedom, several theories of memory emerged in the social sciences and psychoanalysis in the 19th century and the first half of the 20th century. These theories mostly focused on social processes, given widespread distrust that neurology would ever find a physical basis of memory or that one even existed (although Freud, as a neurologist, never abandoned hope).

Dualism remained useful until the middle of the 20th century, when neurology began to make important leaps forward. Nevertheless, many psychoanalysts and social scientists continue to ignore the findings of neuroscience a century later. In some cases, they have built entire edifices on a supposed split between the psychological, linguistic and sociological world, on the one hand, and the physiological, biochemical and electrical functioning of the brain, on the other. Not surprisingly, modern neurological findings about memory tend to be seen as a threat by those who are afraid that neuroscience will force them to abandon their most cherished beliefs. However, it is only possible to defend dualism nowadays by deliberately ignoring the past 50 years of research in molecular biology and genetics, among other fields.

The failure of psychoanalysts, linguists, philosophers and social scientists to engage in interdisciplinary or transdisciplinary debates has had another unfortunate effect. It has encouraged an unquestioning belief among neuroscientists in their ability to locate and explain not only basic memory functions but also more complex memory processes. This goes far beyond the possibilities of neuroscience since it requires hypotheses linking neural functioning to what happens beyond neural networks, for example, to processes of symbolization. Symbolization – our ability to think about our behavior in terms of words and images – is also supported by neural networks but it is not explained by them. The problem is to bridge the gap between a closed causal universe (the physical-chemical-biological) and an open causal universe (the product of symbolization and imagination).

Memory processes do not occur in the physical realm, so they cannot be tracked by technology. They exist beyond the level of neuronal communication, which constitutes only their substrate. Nevertheless, the neurosciences have begun to theorize about memory and symbolization processes, ignoring the philosophical, psychological, linguistic and sociological ideas of the past two centuries – and with the same blinkeredness found in the disciplines just mentioned. Locating the neural substrate of a process, however, is not the same as explaining how it works. Its effects and consequences cannot be detected by any machine. It is a fundamental epistemological mistake to think that finding correlations is same as *explaining*. Often, correlations can be *explained* only at another level of description. Steven Rose (2006) wisely mocks the futility of attempting to register these cerebral events even assuming the existence of an imaginary brain-scope capable of recording all the neuronal communications surrounding any given thought (something that is still far removed from the current possibilities of neuroscience). Assuming that one day such a brain-scope could be built, it would still say nothing about the specific thought processes, which are much more complex than their material support based on neuronal communication.

Leaving aside objections to the term "Neural Darwinism," some of Edelman's hypotheses are truly "illuminating" for understanding memory construction.[6] This is not because he has detected these processes using physical means – that would be impossible. It is because he tries to explain *functions* he cannot detect but which he infers from what he *can* prove and locate. Even though he has not gone about this systematically, his openness to other views – philosophical, psychological and sociological – has been far greater than that of most neuroscientists. Consequently, his work is easier to relate to sociological or psychoanalytical ideas.

The hypothesis of an adaptive neural functioning is particularly useful for understanding the relation between conscious and unconscious systems and their effects on processes of memory construction. This includes the passage from short-term to long-term memory, as well as so-called processes of consolidation of memory, de-learning and the desensitizing effects of terror. These are just a few issues linked to personal, historical and social memory.

Before entering the universe of "Neural Darwinism," a political and ethical rather than epistemological clarification is in order. That we humans – like many other animals – have evolved as social beings by a process of natural selection does not mean that our social *needs* are predetermined. On the contrary, Darwin himself pointed out that the capacity for ethics is a necessary attribute of human nature (Darwin, 1871). This capacity offers us a way of challenging biologically determined social structures.

Emmanuel Levinas, a philosopher and religious thinker who placed ethics in the foreground of his system (Levinas, 1969), famously stated that "Ethics precedes ontology" (ontology is the study of being). Levinas' work itself contains few references to Darwin or evolutionary theory (Atterton, 2011). However, his phrase is a salutary reminder that Darwin's monumental contribution to our understanding of the biological world should not blind us to the terrible consequences of "Social Darwinism." First developed by Herbert Spencer in the late 19th century, Social Darwinism preached the "survival of the fittest" but ignored our equally adaptive capacity for cooperation, which is fundamental for societies to flourish. Darwin himself repeatedly stressed the importance of cooperation.

Henri Bergson – to whom we will return in Chapter 3 – argued that consciousness and memory are fundamentally linked to our need for action, which requires using the past in the present. If we accept that brain function is adaptive, it makes sense to ask how consciousness evolved and which processes support it, as well as which types of action it permits and which it blocks or precludes.

Neuroscience has not yet produced a unified theory of consciousness or the role of memory in consciousness. Nevertheless, some of its hypotheses can usefully be compared with those of psychoanalysis, social sciences and philosophy. These hypotheses concern the effects of memory processes on

Basic memory responses: Habituation, sensitization, conditioning and desensitization[7]

Eric Kandel is currently one of the most famous researchers in memory studies. He has made a fundamental contribution to our understanding of changes in the brain brought about by learning three basic behavioral reactions: (1) *habituation* – we learn not to respond to a stimulus that is presented repeatedly; (2) *sensitization* – a reaction to a stimulus causes an increased reaction to a second stimulus and (3) *classical conditioning* – the transfer of a natural response – for example fear – from one stimulus to a new stimulus.

Working with a simple organism – the sea slug or snail *Aplysia californica* – Kandel studied how information was transmitted between neurons and how the strength of connections between neurons across synapses – the gaps between the neurons – changed. Kandel showed that in short-term memory, only the communication across the synapses is altered. But in long-term memory, the synapses themselves are physically altered. His experiments were simple. Nevertheless, he was able to identify the biochemical substrate of the three behavioral reactions already mentioned – *habituation*, *sensitization* and *classical conditioning* – by studying the synaptic connections and their transformations (Kandel, 2007).

To study *habituation*, a mild (harmless) electric shock was applied to the tail of the sea slug. The slug responded with a strong gill and siphon withdrawal reflex. The transmission of the stimulus was traced through a bundle of axons to the siphon (the "nose" through which the organism breathes). Repeated electrical stimulation was found to decrease the number of dopamine-containing vesicles that released their contents onto the motor neuron by more than 20 times between the first and the tenth stimulus.

The adaptive logic of this response is clear. At first, the nervous system reacts to a stressor with a "fight or flight" response. However, if the stimulus is mild, and there are no other stimuli, the organism eventually becomes habituated and transmission of the stimulus through the neural circuit is gradually reduced. This simple experiment explains, for example, why we can sleep through certain noises (trains, cars, clocks, refrigerators, elevators) to which we have become accustomed even though we find them irritating at first. Habituation can even make such noises necessary, as when city dwellers on vacation complain they cannot sleep because the countryside is too quiet.

The opposite of habituation is *sensitization*. When the stimulus is not mild but painful, the entire nervous system is sensitized to other possible stimuli, as it seeks to generate responses to avoid or cope with the pain. The circuit that is stimulated does not undergo habituation. On the contrary, the reflex strength in another neural pathway is reinforced. This appears to involve serotonin rather than dopamine synaptic transmission. In Kandel's experiments, the entire nervous system of the Aplysia remained sensitized for 30 minutes following the aggressive stimulus until the previous synaptic balance was restored.

Once again, the adaptive purpose of this mechanism is clear: the organism is sensitized to an aggression that may continue or get worse. By activating new "early warning" channels, the organism is able to avoid or confront the aggression more quickly and minimize harm.

Finally, *classical conditioning* explained the results of behavioral psychology experiments at the level of synaptic communication. Kandel showed that new neural pathways are created when a harmless stimulus is repeatedly paired with a painful one. After a while, the organism learns to react to the harmless stimulus without waiting for the painful one. Pavlov had already popularized this type of adaptive response with the classic example of the dog reacting to a sound prior to another event, either pleasant (food) or unpleasant (a punishment).

The enormous synaptic plasticity Kandel discovered in this simple organism, *Aplysia*, leads to hypothesize a fourth possible response to pain: *desensitization*. Although not studied either by Kandel or by behaviorism, this phenomenon is of particular importance in understanding the behavior of concentration camp survivors. Here, I will try to explain the adaptive value of desensitization using the analogy with the three behaviors previously described.

Kandel presents us with three situations:

1 The reiteration of a harmless stimulus (which creates habituation)
2 The appearance of a painful stimulus (which creates sensitization)
3 Pairing of a harmless stimulus and a painful one over time (which creates conditioning)

A fourth variant would be:

4 Permanent exposure to a painful stimulus to which there is no possible reaction (flight or fight is not possible).

What would be the adaptive response at the level of synaptic transmission to this fourth situation? The answer should be: *desensitization*. That is, a damping down of the synaptic transmissions linked to pain, given that pain is only adaptive as an early warning system for action. If action is not possible, then the nervous system should slowly but surely *reduce* the intensity of pain.

In fact, *desensitization* exists at the neurological level and is an important process whereby cells can decrease their sensitivity to a particular neurotransmitter to prevent saturation of the system. Desensitization can be by inactivation, sequestration or degradation of the receptor molecule in a cell membrane, which responds to a particular neurotransmitter. Here is how Squire et al. (2012) explain this phenomenon:

> There are two known mechanisms for desensitization (...). One mechanism is a decrease in response (...) and is quite rapid (seconds to minutes). The other mechanism is the physical removal of receptors from the plasma membrane through a mechanism of receptor-mediated endocytosis [= *actively transporting molecules into the cell*] and tends to require greater periods (minutes to hours). The latter process can be either reversible (sequestration) or irreversible (downregulation), when the receptors are removed from the cell through degradation.
> *(Squire et al., 2012, p. 197)*

Although desensitization appears to be similar to habituation, its functioning is clearly different. Habituation occurs as the result of a specific phenomenon (either a single stimulus or a limited set of stimuli) whose consequences are harmless. Therefore, only the channel affected by the stimulus or stimuli themselves is damped down. Desensitization, on the other hand, occurs in quite different circumstances. The stimuli are often very varied and follow different pathways and systems (there is an almost infinite number of ways to inflict suffering), and they are not harmless. On the contrary, they produce extreme, even unbearable pain. Some consequences of these short-term and long-term mechanisms will be discussed in the following in relation to processes that occur at other levels of explanation, such as the psychic apparatus and social relations.

Desensitization and behavioral inhibition: Henri Laborit's contribution

The inspiration for much neuroscience research into desensitization has undoubtedly been Henri Laborit's (1983) theory of desensitization. Laborit was interested in the relationship between somatic pathologies and stress. He administered electrical shocks to mice and compared the stress levels in those that were allowed to escape and those that were not. Mice are more complex than Kandel's *Aplysia californica* and better models for human behavior because they are mammals.

Laborit found that cortisol and other glucocorticoids – hormones that normally help our bodies cope with stress – gradually destroy the immune system if anxiety is prolonged. He also found that after a time, those mice that were *not* allowed to escape developed behavioral inhibition. They would not leave the cage even when they were free to go.

When faced danger, we normally have two options: "fight or flight." However, when neither is possible – as in the case of a prison or a concentration camp – a third response appears: behavioral inhibition. Behavioral inhibition implies waiting in a state of tension, restraining the impulse to act even though one's body is ready for action. The stimulus is not inhibited, only a response that is considered inappropriate.

At the emotional level, Laborit accordingly distinguished between fear – our basic response to danger – and what he called *angoisse*, which corresponds more or less to the notion of chronic anxiety. For Laborit, *angoisse* results from a state of uncertainty, where a danger cannot be predicted or no previous response pattern exists to direct action. Serious problems occur when a state of panic is sustained over time. Too much cortisol over a period of time can suppress the immune system, increase blood pressure and sugar, among other problems. Many chronically depressed patients have high blood levels of cortisol.

As Laborit points out: "While the anxious individual waits and hopes for the time to take action, the depressed individual seems to have lost even this hope" (Laborit, 1983, p. 59).

This process of adaptive desensitization and behavioral inhibition is obviously relevant to understanding the experience of concentration camp inmates subjected to a system that is arbitrary, clandestine and therefore terrifying. In the second half of the 1970s, for example, anyone in Argentina could be classified as a subversive criminal (or, to quote one Argentine perpetrator, "complicit, sympathetic, indifferent or timid" [8]) and subjected to a systematic regime of suffering in which "flight or fight" was impossible.

The construction of long-term memory: Repetition and affect

Kandel made another important discovery that is useful for understanding memory processes and that concerns the way short-term memory passes into long-term memory. The different types of learning already mentioned (habituation, sensitization, classical conditioning) occur at the level of chemical connections through neurotransmitters. At this level, there is little or no creation of new connections, but simply a weakening, strengthening or interconnection of existing circuits. In contrast, long-term memory requires establishing new pathways of connection. Kandel assumed that the biochemical pathway could not be the same, but required the involvement of genes to create new pathways.

Kandel's research revealed mechanisms involving gene transcription and protein formation within the nucleus of sensory neurons leading to long-lasting cellular changes, including the creation of new synapses. This amazing and complex process uses different regulators of gene transcription: activators and repressors. Activators encode the proteins that switch genes on, while repressors encode the proteins that switch genes off. Following Jacob and Monod's model of gene expression and regulation, Kandel and Dusan Bartsch discovered that these distinct phases of gene activation and deactivation are exemplified most clearly in two forms of the CREB protein. CREB-1 protein activates gene expression in the neuronal nucleus, while CREB-2 protein deactivates it.

At the risk of oversimplification, the process is as follows. In his *Aplysia* experiments, Kandel found that repeated stimulation of synaptic connections causes two types of proteins to enter the cell nucleus: protein kinase A and MAP kinase. Protein kinase A activates CREB-1, while the MAP kinase deactivates CREB-2. Therefore, the creation of new synaptic connections requires not only the activation of certain gene expression but also the simultaneous deactivation of the protein that prevents this happening.

Although complex, the process is – once again – peculiarly adaptive. Contrary to the assumptions of some philosophers, psychologists and even poets, we could not possibly remember *all* our experiences and impressions because our brains would not be able to store so much information. The need for simultaneous activation and deactivation of different genes makes it more difficult for short-term memory to be transformed accidentally into long-term memory. This ensures we do not end up like *Funes the Memorious*, the fictional character in Borges' short story of the same name, who could remember every unimportant fact in his life, but needed a whole day to remember the previous one. Luckily for most of us, over-remembering (or hyperthymesia) is a rare condition resulting from a brain dysfunction.

How, then, are long-term memories created? There are only three ways that information can move from short-term memory to long-term memory: repetition, association and urgency. Repetition is the most familiar learning method. It is used to memorize multiplication tables and to create the motor routines needed to drive a vehicle, or play a piece of music. Repeated stimulation of the same connection releases the proteins needed not only to activate some genes but also to deactivate others, allowing the creation of new proteins and the establishment of new synaptic connections.

Association allows a new piece of information to be learned more quickly by tapping into an existing neural connection. For example, I might memorize my passport number by relating it to the dates of some historical events.

Urgency, on the other hand, involves the release of stress hormones, which instantly strengthen the connections between synapses. Kandel cites the example of a car accident. Here, the intense emotion probably causes a large number of MAP kinase molecules to be sent to the nucleus, inhibiting all the CREB-2 molecules and allowing protein kinase A to activate CREB-1 instantly. According to Kandel, this process would explain the vividness of intensely emotional memories that return like flashes as if a detailed image had been etched instantly on the brain.

Without going into the specifics of gene functioning, it is clear that these ways of encoding long-term memories are qualitatively different. Emotion affects both how and where the brain encodes the information. It can create vivid and detailed memories but the encoding or labeling of the event – the ability to recall or retrieve the memory – is not under conscious control. For example, I may still become anxious when I see where I had my car accident even if I do not consciously remember it. In short, it is more or less accepted that two brain structures are involved in long-term memory: the amygdala encodes emotional memories, while the hippocampus-cortex deals with the rest.

However, that is not all. One factor that complicates memory studies is that most learning is unconscious:

1 Motor skills seem to become automatic once they are encoded (i.e., complex routines can be performed without conscious thought or attention, making it possible to simultaneously perform another activity – for example, engaging in a conversation while driving a car). Nevertheless, automatic routines can usually be brought under conscious control (for example, in an emergency).
2 In contrast, most emotional, fear-related memories are encoded with an emotional, not a narrative marker, and are therefore difficult to retrieve. Moreover, their access to consciousness may be suppressed as a protective mechanism. An understanding of this process at the neurological level could help understand the functioning of the unconscious mind, as theorized by Freud. Presumably, repression happens when the emotion is so strong that it could disrupt the person's identity. Now, repression is not a neurological concept but a psychological one. Nevertheless, it could (and should, according to Freud) be mediated by a neural process that would allow it to be observed, even though we would not be observing "the unconscious" itself but only the biological substrate.

What happens, then, when an emotional memory is denied access to consciousness? As the term "motion" suggests, an emotion is an impulse to act. For example, fear forces us to choose between fight and flight. However, when access to consciousness is blocked, emotion may act in ways the individual cannot explain: through phobias, obsessions, failures, jokes, forgetfulness and, especially, repetition compulsion – in short, through Freud's repertoire of psychopathological behaviors. But let's not get ahead of ourselves: we will return to this subject in the next chapter.

Neural Darwinism: From memory to consciousness

We will move on now from the construction of long-term memory to the problem of consciousness. Although the two are linked, they are quite different issues. Current neuroscience theories of memory formation have a lot of empirical support, whereas theories of consciousness are much more speculative – although the memory processes already outlined above may lend more weight to these speculations.

Edelman's theory of "Neural Darwinism" starts from the observation that the human nervous system is made up of around 10^{11} neurons, each connected to thousands of other neurons, whereas the human genome comprises only 20,000 genes (Henniger, 2012). It is therefore impossible for the human genome to encode the wiring of the whole brain in detail. To explain how genes construct our brains, Edelman calls on the Darwin's concepts of variation and selection.

Edelman argues that there are three fundamental types of selection. First, *developmental selection* during the biological development of the embryo creates a primary repertoire of structurally variant neuronal groups capable of performing quite different functions. After birth, *experiential selection* occurs as a result of life experiences and interaction with the social world. This gives rise to a secondary repertoire of neuronal circuits created by changes in the strength of the connections or synapses. Finally, *reentrant signaling* sends signals back and forth between neuronal groups by means of so-called reentrant connections. According to Edelman, information in the brain is distributed among many "maps" and these maps speak to one another in order to create categories of things and events, or to establish temporal and spatial relationships between separate items. The brain strengthens new "maps" that are successful and eliminates those that are not.

Together, these three principles of brain functioning provide a powerful means to understanding the key neuronal interactions required for the formation of a memory, as well as the role that memory plays in consciousness.

Due to its complexity, Edelman's theory has not been fully validated although Edelman himself claims it is supported by extensive neural modeling (Edelman, 1993). Nevertheless, it may serve to support ideas from other disciplines such as phenomenology on the functions of memory processes. A comparison between Edelman's theories and Sir Frederic Charles Bartlett's findings from the early 20th century is highly revealing. A forerunner of cognitive as well as cultural psychology, Bartlett (1995 [1932]) asked individuals to reproduce narratives, drawings, informative texts, etc., after a time lapse. He showed that memory is, in fact, a reconstruction and that gaps are filled in with material from previous experiences. It is interesting to compare Bartlett's results with Edelman's hypotheses, produced almost a century later. We will return to Bartlett in Chapter 3.

Consciousness and "reentrant" processes

Edelman explains the emergence and development of consciousness in terms of two interconnected hypotheses: the already mentioned *reentrant signaling* between neural maps, and a *dynamic nucleus* of neuronal communication (discussed in the next section). Notice that in this model, there is no "homunculus" or central coordinating area in the brain. Instead, various maps are simply excited at the same time, activating millions of neurons in parallel, which in turn activate other maps that also comprise millions of neurons. It is through this process of "reentry" that perceptions, motor behaviors, conceptual thought and consciousness come into being (Changeux, 2012).

The *reentrant signaling* hypothesis is based on the consensus among most neuroscientific currents that consciousness (like memory) does not have a specific location in the brain but involves the interaction of numerous areas scattered throughout the cortical thalamus system, and possibly other sectors of the brain. To explain how these areas interact, Edelman uses the concept of large-scale reentry processes. However, he points out that "the activity patterns of the groups of neurons that support conscious experience must be constantly changing and sufficiently differentiated from each other." Otherwise, "If a large number of neurons in the brain start firing in the same way, reducing the diversity of the brain's neuronal repertoires, as is the case in deep sleep and epilepsy, consciousness disappears" (Edelman & Tononi, 2000, p. 36).

Reentry processes, then, sustain consciousness process by coordinating different brain areas and functions – for example, perceptual processes in the thalamus-cortical system; performance or planning in the pre-frontal cortex; or the consolidation of short-term memory into long-term memory in the hippocampus. These different subsystems allow the performance of a complex variety of routines, both motor and cognitive, while reentry processes coordinate them and exchange information between the different subsystems. In Edelman's own words:

> Reentry allows an animal with a variable and uniquely individual nervous system to partition an unlabeled world into objects and events in the absence of a homunculus or computer program. As we have already discussed, reentry leads to the synchronization of the activity of neuronal groups in different brain maps, binding them into circuits capable of temporally coherent output. Reentry is thus the central mechanism by which the spatiotemporal coordination of diverse sensory and motor events takes place.
>
> *(Edelman & Tononi, 2000, p. 85)*

The *reentrant signaling* hypothesis explains the qualitative difference between the brain and a digital computer. Digital computers work on a binary system where "0" represents off and "1" represents on. By grouping these "bits" ("0" and "1") into larger chunks, an almost infinite number of combinations is possible. A computer receives inputs that it must match to previously coded variables held in its memory. Nevertheless, binary computers have serious limitations. In particular, they are unable to handle ambiguous data that cannot be classified in terms of "on"/"off." The only way that computational logic can deal with ambiguity is by pre-programming the machines with an infinite number of possible matches. However, in real life, it is impossible for all inputs to be known and classified in advance. Life is qualitatively different from the artificial reality created by computer software.

Following Edelman, Kandel defines the brain as "a machine for resolving ambiguities" and so quite different from a computer. This explains why its processes are much more chemical than electrical. Chemical signals can process input from the world by activating, reinforcing, inhibiting or creating new synaptic connections. On the other hand, electrical signals allow reflex actions to occur relatively quickly, but are much less flexible. In other words, the chemical universe is not only structured in terms of "on/off" but also takes into account intensity and change.

Unlike what happens with computers, the stimuli that living organisms receive from the natural and/or social world are not coded in advance. They are potentially ambiguous and context-dependent. They are not usually accompanied by prior judgements about their meaning or labels that allow them to be included in classification systems. Moreover, computer models of the brain fail to explain how basic classification systems are constructed – those responsible for structuring the whole – unless, of course, God programs them with information about the "real" world. Fortunately, the structure of our brains is *not* pre-determined, but reflects the essentially "selective" and adaptive nature of life as theorized by Darwin.

Brain structure is not predetermined or fixed, then, but plastic and dynamic. It is also what biologists call "degenerate" in the sense that structurally dissimilar components/modules/pathways can perform similar functions (i.e. are effectively interchangeable) under certain conditions, but perform distinct functions in other conditions. This so-called "degeneracy" allows a system to produce the same results through different processes, making a central processor unnecessary. "Degeneracy" (functional redundancy) should not be confused with "degeneration," which means a change from a more complex to a simpler, less differentiated form as a result of less varied or less complex conditions of life. Both terms may sound negative to readers coming from the social sciences or otherwise committed to fighting racism. However, neither has a negative meaning in biology. On the contrary, "degeneracy" holds an enormous evolutionary advantage by providing robustness against brain damage, while "degeneration" is neutral.

The fact that problems can be solved in different ways means that successful solutions to problems will reinforce connections in the brain, while unsuccessful solutions will inhibit them (although these connections remain available for other possible uses). This makes it more likely that that the successful solutions will be repeated to solve similar problems in future. However, if these solutions fail to work for whatever reason – perhaps because the problems are different, other solutions may be activated and prioritized.

One result of neural plasticity is that errors play a very different role in biological as opposed to computational systems. In a computer program, errors must be debugged in order to make the system more efficient or prevent it from "freezing." In a biological system, errors are stored and analyzed because they may lead to more effective solutions to new problems that arise as reality becomes more complex. In other words, biological systems like the human brain are capable of learning from their mistakes.

In the "Neural Darwinism" hypothesis, it is reentry processes – that is, intercommunications between neuronal circuits – that promote learning. They do so by selecting the most appropriate responses to sets of stimuli. These responses are not preprogrammed or hardwired into the brain, but arise out of interactions between the subject and the stimuli through the perceptual system and its diverse and complex links with the sensory-motor systems. Sensory-motor systems develop as children gain use and coordination of their muscles (motor development), and experience the environment through input from the senses.

The psychogenetic epistemology created after the discoveries of the developmental psychology has explored in considerable depth the links between the knowing subject and the stimuli that come from reality. In particular, Jean Piaget's pioneering work explained cognitive development in terms of processes that adapt new input to fit existing knowledge (assimilation) or – where this is not possible – adapt existing knowledge to fit new input (accommodation). However, assimilation is the norm because it leads to equilibration and reduces frustration (Piaget, 1985). Developmental psychology attempts to explain the interaction between subject and stimuli in terms of developmental stages, each defined by increasing complex connections between perceptual and sensorimotor systems, and symbolization processes. Piaget's work on child development – like that of his contemporary Bartlett on memory – is fully compatible with the self-structuring system described by Edelman. Indeed, Edelman's work on brain functioning provides valuable support for both Piaget's and later cognitive theories about the interaction between subject and object, the knower and the known.

Returning now to the central theme of this volume, memory processes, Edelman describes consciousness as a "remembered present" that makes sense in the here and now of past events and/or stimuli together with the most effective responses in dealing with them. In this regard, Edelman says:

> We stress repetition after some time in this definition because it is the ability to re-create an act separated by a certain duration from the original signal set that is characteristic of memory. And in mentioning a changing

context, we pay heed to a key property of memory in the brain: that it is, in some sense, a form of constructive recategorization during ongoing experience, rather than a precise replication of a previous sequence of events.
(Edelman & Tononi, 2000, p. 95)

In fact, Edelman's idea that memory is a constructive recategorization during ongoing experience has become mainstream in neuroscience. The fact that no physical substrate for "memory" has been found and that memories may change each time they are recalled into consciousness lends weight to the idea of memory as a construction bringing together structures and processes scattered throughout the brain. Memory seeks to create coherence, a pattern that precludes other possible patterns (Edelman & Tononi, 2000, p. 147) and is linked to processes of "attention." These processes are able to select a particular group from the almost infinite and chaotic set of ambiguous stimuli that each living being is permanently subjected to.

Here, it is worth pointing out that our memory traces cannot simply be a record of our various experiences of the world or the drives coming from our own bodies. They must also include *imagined* events and our *reflections* on our experiences. These memory traces would also be produced by a combination or mixture of processes. They would be stored not as permanent recordings in a particular part of the brain, but rather as synaptic connections that are updated and transformed each time they are reused (for example, when a memory is recalled).

The dynamic nucleus hypothesis

The second of Edelman's ideas to explain the emergence and development of consciousness is the "dynamic nucleus hypothesis." According to Edelman, the dynamic nucleus is created by the interaction of large numbers of neuronal subsystems and allows for the emergence of subjectivity – an "I." All stimuli, perceptions and action routines produce a neuronal response. Consciousness would be the collective interaction of some of these subsystems through multiple, complex reentry processes occurring over and over again in hundreds of milliseconds.

It is reasonable to suppose that what Freud called the "conscious system" and "unconscious system" would be determined by their integration into, or disconnection from, the dynamic nucleus. Nevertheless, authors such as Ansermet and Magistretti (2004) use the term "unconscious system" only in its Freudian sense, preferring to describe the "disconnected" sectors as *nonconscious*. This notion would be compatible with Kandel's findings on the effect of emotion on the long-term memory.

As mentioned earlier, skills become unconscious with practice. Motor routines and skills need to be learned consciously if they are to be effective.

This is the process by which we first learn to ride a bicycle, drive a car or play a particularly difficult musical passage. At first, it is necessary to break the problem down and choose which subskill(s) to focus on. However, once mastered, motor routines and skills are much more efficient when controlled by unconscious, implicit processes. For the most part, they can run automatically, independently of distractions and momentary lapses in attention. This frees up consciousness for other functions and explains why it is possible for an experienced motorist – but not a learner – to drive a car and hold a complex conversation at the same time. The learner still needs to focus consciously on the road.

Although Edelman stops here, his "dynamic nucleus hypothesis" could be extended – with a little help from Kandel – to explore the problem of trauma. Here, consciousness and unconsciousness take on a more Freudian meaning. We will be examining Freud's work in Chapter 2. Sigmund Freud spoke of the need for a "stimulus shield" – a set of filters that protects our senses from being overwhelmed by excessive stimuli (Freud, 1955 [1920]). Now, if consciousness is a system that allows different stimuli to be integrated into the structure of the self, some experiences are just too traumatic to be assimilated coherently into our perceived identity or self-image. Nevertheless, they have enough emotional impact to be recorded in long-term memory. For this to happen, however, they must follow an unconscious route, which is how Kandel claims all emotional experiences are recorded.

For the moment, the main thing to remember is that experiences perceived as threats to our identity are not integrated into the dynamic nucleus that makes up consciousness. Nietzsche expressed this discrepancy with a certain irony: "I have done that," says my memory. "I cannot have done that" says my pride and remains unshakeable. Finally – memory yields" (Nietzsche, 1989 [1886], p. 86). Freud took this phrase from Nietzsche to develop his own ideas about repression. Repression will be dealt with in detail in the next chapter. For the time being, I simply wish to point out the similarity between the neuroscientific and psychoanalytic approaches to implicit memory – that is, long-term memories that are acquired and used unconsciously. As Edelman's theory suggests, these memories continue to operate autonomously, establishing relationships with other subsystems (sensorimotor, perception, language, etc.) without passing through the dynamic nucleus, and in ways that are outside our conscious control.

Freud and his disciples believed traumatic memories were responsible for hysterias, phobias and "repetition compulsion" (an unconscious tendency to repeat destructive or painful actions). They also believed that trauma could be made conscious, reflected upon and resignified. In this way, these memories could be brought under voluntary control. For Freud, the "working through" of repressed or buried trauma required "word-representation." As Freud himself put it:

> The conscious representation comprises the thing-representation [*Sachvorstellung*] plus the corresponding word-representation [*plus der zugehörigen Wortstellung*], the unconscious one consist of the thing-representation alone.
> *(Freud, 1953–1966, Volume XIV, 201)*

In Edelman's terms, language allowed some of the subsystems that were outside conscious control to connect with the dynamic nucleus. Language is what Edelman calls "consciousness of a superior order," existing only in humans and some primates.

Without going into detail about Freud's ideas on the functioning of the psychic apparatus, it is clear that Edelman's reentry and dynamic nucleus hypotheses provide a possible biological substrate for psychoanalysis in general and memory processes in particular. In fact, Freud abandoned his search for biological explanations after writing *Psychology for Neurologists* at the end of the 19th century because of the limitations of the science of his time. The current state of neuroscience in the 21st century will perhaps allow us to pick up where Freud left off.

Memory as the area in which meaning is constructed

Action precedes understanding. We do many more things than we are aware of, just as we know much more than we think we know. Understanding is not a prerequisite for action, but it is an excellent tool for reflecting on and determining our responsibility for our actions. The ability to critically analyze our interactions with the natural and social world is a high-water mark in our development of conscious awareness, and memory plays a crucial role in this ability.

As previously mentioned, perceptual stimuli neither enter the nervous system with labels attached to them, nor is the brain hardwired to classify them. Nevertheless, neuroscience distinguishes an ever-growing number of memory systems. These include memories related to sensory perception (auditory, visual, gustatory, olfactory and tactile memories), sensory-motor and procedural knowledge (motor skills), or language. These in turn can be classified functionally as episodic memories (recall of personal experiences) or semantic memories (recall of general facts about the world), among others.

It is likely that over the years, new memory systems will continue to be discovered and classified, as well as subsystems with different levels of interconnection and integration. It must be emphasized, however, that subsystems are "non-representational." That is, they do not record events and reproduce them. They simply keep a record of how certain stimuli activate them. When they detect similar stimuli, they generate sets of responses through the reentry processes already described. These more or less physically traceable memories are thus chaotic, scattered and meaningless in themselves. None of them is a "representation" as such and they are not a "memory" in the sense usually given to the term in the social sciences or history, but rather fragmentary and primitive parts of a memory.

In this work, I use the term "memory processes" to describe attempts to impose meaning on the chaos of perceptions and fragmentary memories in the various subsystems. As we will see, this is done by creating a "remembered present" through a process of constructing "scenes." A "scene" is a reconstruction in which groups of perceptions and stimuli are linked together and given a meaning, a coherence that is not found in reality – or rather, in our experience of reality. On the contrary, its purpose is to integrate sets of stimuli and perceptions with a given set of actions that are also registered in sensory-motor subsystems.

From this perspective, memory is not simply a video recording of past events to be passively replayed; it is a profoundly creative activity. Every act of memory is an act of the imagination. Bergson's ideas on different forms of memory published in *Matter and Memory* (Bergson, 1911) at the end of the 19th century were provocative – for example, his notion that being conscious of something means looking at it in the light of the past. Today, it could be said that neuroscience has gone a step further in suggesting that Bergson's "image-remembrance" – what is usually recognized as "memory" – is a creative and radically new act that attempts to give coherence and meaning to the chaos of stimuli that are located in certain physical substrates of brain functioning.

In neuroscientific terms, it could be hypothesized that *meaning* is created in the dynamic nucleus when various subsystems of perceptions, stimuli and motor activities are brought together and given a coherent explanation that they do not possess separately. This narrative meaning makes actions more efficient by providing goals, and a degree of stability and permanence to the processes of identity formation, which – as the term identity suggests – require high levels of internal consistency.

The "I" as a construction of the self is found in higher primates (for example, chimpanzees) as well as humans. It allows for what Edelman calls "consciousness of a superior order" – *the consciousness of being conscious*, the consciousness of our own existence as living beings different from other beings and the environment. However, this "higher-order" consciousness permanently seeks coherence. This is demonstrated not only by our philosophical need for a subject but also by our conscious attempts to adjust to different anomalies or inconsistencies. The study of these attempts has been a fundamental focus of neuroscience for decades and has given rise to a large number of hypotheses.

Two examples will suffice to illustrate these processes: binocular fusion, the merging of slightly different images from the two eyes; and anosognosia, a condition resulting from brain damage in which a person with a disability is unaware of having it. Anosognosia is sometimes accompanied by asomatognosia, in which patients deny ownership of body parts such as their limbs.

In the case of binocular fusion, it should be noted that if the images presented to each eye are incongruous – for example an object shown to the right eye is completely different from that shown to the left eye – binocular fusion becomes impossible. However, instead of going blind or mad, experimental subjects report seeing one or other of the objects before their eyes alternately, with one of the two stimuli being eliminated automatically (binocular rivalry). Thus, perception chooses between fusion and suppression depending on which provides greater coherence and thus proves more adaptive.

The case of asomatognosia is even more interesting. As a response to the lack of sensation in a limb, perhaps due to paralysis, patients usually deny that the affected limb belongs to their body before accepting their loss. According to Edelman:

> [A]fter a massive stroke or surgical resection, a conscious human being is rapidly "resynthesized" or reunified within the limits of a new, solipsistic universe that, to outside appearances, is warped and restricted. The network of relations that make up a conscious event is not left broken and discontinuous; rather, the loose ends tend rapidly to cohere again and bridge the rupture. The drive to integration is so strong that often no empty space is perceived where there is, in fact, a frightening gap. Apparently, the feeling of an absence is far less tolerable than the absence of a feeling.
>
> *(Edelman & Tononi, 2000, p. 29)*

The possibly adaptive nature of desensitization has already been mentioned in relation to Kandel's studies. Arguably, desensitization occurs not only in response to physical trauma but also to emotional loss. It explains the numbness that accompanies the process of melancholia, a process defined by Freud as an attempt to repair a loss that the ego finds unbearable. This numbness is especially acute when grief is blocked.

Most brain injuries produce a similar response. Unlike what happens with a computer, where a failure can cause the system to freeze, reboot or stop functioning altogether, either new brain cells are created to replace the damaged ones or different parts of the brain are reorganized/rewired. This reorganization is possible due to the "degeneracy" (i.e. redundancy) of the system already mentioned. However, the most interesting aspect of the way in which the brain repairs itself is its attempt to restore coherence by resignifying ongoing experience. This guarantees the most-effective behavior possible for the amount of damage involved. This wonderful adaptive strategy is what differentiates selectionist mechanisms from conventional computers, and is what Edelman means by "Neural Darwinism."

In the light of all this, it is therefore necessary to revise the idea of memory as a "record" or an "imprint." This idea, which has run through Western philosophy since Aristotle, influenced the psychoanalytic notion of a "mnemonic imprint" to the extent that some authors still assume that trauma involves a literal record of a traumatic event. The metaphor chosen by Edelman to refute this notion is extremely powerful: rejecting the ancient metaphor of memory as a representational inscription (in wax or stone), he writes:

> A nonrepresentational memory would be like changes in a glacier influenced by changes in the weather ... the melting and refreezing of the glacier represent changes in the synaptic response, the ensuing different rivulets descending the mountain represent the neural pathways, and the pond into which they feed represents the output ...
> *(Edelman, 2004, xiii)*

In other words, memory is not a relatively permanent imprint; it is a process that is repeated again and again with a different result each time, even if the raw materials are similar. When we remember a scene, we produce a "remembered present." But when we recall it for a third, fourth or fifth time, we really return to the last time that we remembered the scene, the last act of remembering and not to the original experience. The glacier melts and freezes each time a memory is recalled, but the materials from which it is reassembled always come from the most recent melting. They derive from the original elements, yet they are slightly different from them. The previous memory states can no longer be accessed once a new "remembering" has taken place.

Edelman's non-representational model of memory ties in well with Freud's ideas on the difference between how memory works in the conscious and the unconscious system. Although Freud uses the term "memory imprint"[9] in many of his works, in *Beyond the Pleasure Principle* (Freud, 1955 [1920]) he argues that the only unprocessed images (representations, stimuli) we have from our past are those preserved in the unconscious. These images were never consciously recalled or given a meaning, and so were never integrated into a narrative system (fundamental operation of the conscious system). Freud states:

> Though this may not be an absolutely binding consideration, it may at any rate lead us to conjecture that becoming conscious and leaving behind a memory-trace are processes incompatible with each other in the same system. We should thus be able to say: in the system Bw. [the system that produces consciousness] the process of excitation becomes conscious but

it leaves behind no lasting trace; all the traces of it on which memory relies would come about in the next systems inwards from the propagation of the excitation on to them.

(Freud, 1955 [1920], p. 28)

In other words, Freud suggests that as soon as these imprints are accessed and integrated into the consciousness, they become meaningful and disappear.

Although Freud himself introduces this idea as a "conjecture," it is fully compatible with Edelman's notion that conscious memory is nonrepresentational. Moreover, Freud explains that trauma cannot be forgotten precisely because it cannot be remembered – at least, not intentionally. The traumatic event continues to operate with the same force as when it was first perceived because its lack of integration into consciousness prevents it from "melting." Occasionally, it manages to pass through what Freud calls in this same work "the defensive measures of the barrier against stimuli." Freud concluded the paragraph by saying something even more suggestive than Edelman's own metaphor:

If one reflects how little we know from other sources about the origin of consciousness, the pronouncement that *consciousness arises in the place of the memory-trace* must be conceded at least the importance of a statement which is to some extent definite.

(Freud, 1955 [1920], p. 28)

Edelman's and Kandel's work provide the neurological evidence that Freud himself searched for his whole life to support his intuitions. Unfortunately, physiological psychology, the forerunner of neuroscience, was dominated in Freud's lifetime by phrenology and the notion of a physical location of memory. It could not even imagine the real complexity of brain functioning with its infinite number of interconnected networks.

For Israel Rosenfield, a neurologist who continued Edelman's work, every interpretation is in fact a process of *creation* (Rosenfield, 1988, 1992). In a critique of Freud's interpretation of dreams, Rosenfield suggests that dreams are not deformed or condensed versions of memory. They are the real way in which images exist (chaotic, disordered and incoherent) in the brain. Rosenfield claims that these images or stimuli acquire meaning in representations by interacting with a context and the need for action. In dreams, when they are freed from the need for coherence, they appear exactly as they were recorded – chaotically. In dreams, they lack the meaning that the conscious apparatus attributes to them. It is only when we are awake that we try to construct *some sort of meaning* from these images coming from layers of primitive memory. For Rosenfield, memory would be the capacity to "interpret" this chaos of confused perceptions and images. This interpretation is carried out by linking the past with the present and giving it a meaning.

It is possible, then, to define *memory processes* as an attempt to construct meaning from a set of past stimuli and sensations recorded throughout different perceptual systems and linked to the present through action. These are given coherence through interactions with one another. When we reconstruct a memory, we simultaneously create a conscious subject that relates to these dispersed elements from the past. By constructing a scene, a "remembered present" in which a narrative of the self emerges, we construct an identity for ourselves. This narrative of self does not arise only from our own perceptions and representations. We all carry around in our heads a mental picture of our predecessors and contemporaries, as well as a vision of our descendants.

To summarize the main points of this chapter once again, neuroscience has contributed significantly to our understanding of memory although not all of its hypotheses have been confirmed. It has shown that memory is not a literal reproduction of the past, but instead relies on constructive processes. Memory representations are linked adaptively to the search for meaning. At the same time, we have seen that the logical adaptive response to extreme and prolonged suffering such as that experienced in a concentration camp could be a progressive desensitization.

This raises questions at a different level of explanation – the socio-political one. What types of memory processes or representations are consistent with subjective obliteration and desensitization? Does desensitization lead merely to repression and silence, or can it be expressed in narrative structures that seek to reconstruct a coherent identity, filling the void left by repression with "acceptable" stories? Is such a reconstruction viable or, on the contrary, does it operate by desubjectivizing narrative identity? How can these processes be linked to awareness? How can we describe the relationship between interindividual processes and the construction of collective narratives such as myths or history?

Some of these questions cannot be answered by neuroscience, even though neuroscientific discoveries have provided even stronger reasons for asking them. It is therefore essential to move to another level – the "psychic structure" – if we wish to unravel the construction of memory representation and the problems caused by the impact of trauma.

Notes

1 For an account of neurologists and psychiatrists' work on CIA projects during the Cold War, see also Naomi Klein's (2007) chilling but brilliant journalistic work, *The Shock Doctrine. The Rise of Disaster Capitalism.*
2 Gerald Edelman shared the 1972 Nobel Prize in Physiology or Medicine for his work on the chemical structure of antibody molecules. Following his discoveries about the selective nature of the functioning of the antibody system, he devoted his subsequent work to the study of the brain. At the end of the seventies, he coined the notion of "Neural Darwinism" which inspired one of the important currents of neuroscientific development. He carried out numerous studies, first

at Rockefeller University and then at the Scripps Neuroscience Institute in San Diego. This chapter follows the reasoning of Edelman's later texts, and takes many of the quotes from the work he co-authored with Giulio Tononi under the title *The Universe of Consciousness. How Matter Becomes Imagination* (Edelman & Tononi, 2000). However, for a more exhaustive follow-up of Edelman's work, it is essential to consult at least three previous works: *Neural Darwinism* (1990), *The Remembered Present* (1989) and *Bright Air, Brilliant Fire* (1992). For his more philosophical conclusions, two more recent works have been consulted: *Wider than the Sky. The Phenomenal Gift of Consciousness* (2004) and *Second Nature. Brain Science and Human Knowledge* (2006).

3 Eric Kandel was born in Vienna in 1929. He emigrated to the United States in 1939, when he was not yet 10 years old, to escape the Nazis. Later, he carried out fundamental research for the study of memory processes. He received the Nobel Prize for Medicine in 2000 for his discoveries on the transmission of signals in the nervous system. Since 1974, he has been a member of the National Academy of Sciences of the United States.

4 Jean-Pierre Changeux completed his doctoral studies at the Institut Pasteur, under the direction of Jacques Monod and François Jacob, authors who are fundamental to the development of contemporary genetics. In 1967, he joined Monod's own chair of molecular biology. In 1972, he was appointed Director of the Molecular Biology Unit at the Institut Pasteur and in 1975 a member of the Collège de France. One of his fundamental research topics has been the relationship between the brain and thought. Among his latest books are *The Good, the True, and the Beautiful: A Neuronal Approach.* (2012); and *The Physiology of Truth. Neuroscience and Human Knowledge* (2009). In particular, his concept of "selective synapse stabilization" echoes many of Edelman's and Kandel's ideas. Nevertheless, I cite Edelman and Kandel sparingly in order not to overburden the reader with unnecessary technicalities in what is already a dense chapter.

5 This work repeatedly addresses the question of consciousness, both from a neuroscientific and a psychoanalytical perspective (in the distinction between the conscious, preconscious and unconscious apparatus) and with respect to the philosophical and socio-political derivations of such analysis. It should be clarified that I do not accept the distinction made by some neuroscientific authors such as Adam Zeman (2006) between "consciousness" and "awareness." Here I will define consciousness as the "immediate knowledge that subjects have of themselves, their acts and reflections." It should not be confused with Freud's "conscious apparatus," which is also referred to in this book.

6 The term "Neural Darwinism" has been criticized on the basis that neuronal groups are instructed by the environment rather than undergoing blind variation (Crick, 1989).

7 Although the analysis on the processes of desensitization is my own, I have subsequently found some particularly enlightening suggestions in John Bowlby's brilliant "Attachment and Loss" trilogy, especially Volume 2: *Separation: Anxiety and Anger* (Bowlby, 1973).

8 The declarations were made by the former de facto governor of the province of Buenos Aires, Ibérico Saint Jean, in 1977, saying "First we will kill all the subversives; then we will kill their collaborators; then ... their sympathizers. Then ... those who remain indifferent; and finally we will kill the timid." Published in the *International Herald Tribune*, May 26, 1977.

9 The Standard Edition translates "Erinnerungs-" (sometimes "Gedächtnis-") in compound nouns with the English adjective "mnemic" even though "memory" is identical to the original in register.

References

Ansermet, F., & Magistretti, P. (2004). *Biology of freedom: Neural plasticity, experience, and the unconscious* (S. Fairfield, Trans). Other Press.
Atterton, P. (2011). Nourishing the hunger of the other: A rapprochement between Levinas and Darwin. *Symploke, 19*(1), 17–33. Project MUSE, www.muse.jhu.edu/article/463483
Bartlett, F. (1995) [1932]. *Remembering. A study in experimental and social psychology*. Cambridge University Press.
Bergson, H. (1911). *Matter and memory* (N. M. Paul & W. S. Palmer, Trans.), George Allen & Co. https://doi.org/10.1037/13803-000
Bowlby, J. (1973). *Attachment and loss* (3 vols.). Basic Books.
Changeux, J. P. (2009). *The physiology of truth. neuroscience and human knowledge*. Harvard University Press.
Changeux, J. P. (2012). *The good, the true, and the beautiful: A neuronal approach* (L. Garey, Trans.). Yale University Press.
Crick, F. (1989). Neural Edelmanism. *Trends in Neuroscience, 12*(7), 240–248. https://doi.org/10.1016/0166-2236(89)90019-2
Darwin, C. (1871). *The descent of man* (1st ed.). Murray.
Edelman, G. M. (1989). *The remembered present*. Basic Books.
Edelman, G. M. (1990). *Neural Darwinism*. Oxford Paperbacks.
Edelman, G. M. (1992). *Bright air, brilliant fire*. Basic Books.
Edelman, G. M. (1993). Neural Darwinism: Selection and reentrant signaling in higher brain function. *Neuron, 10*, 115–125.
Edelman, G. M. (2004). *Wider than the sky. The phenomenal gift of consciousness*. Yale University Press.
Edelman, G. M. (2006). *Second nature. Brain science and human knowledge*. Yale University Press.
Edelman, G. M., & Tononi, G. (2000). *A universe of consciousness: How matter becomes imagination*. Basic Books.
Feierstein, D. (2000). *Seis estudios sobre genocidio. Análisis de las relaciones sociales: otredad, exclusion, exterminio*. EUDEBA.
Feierstein, D. (2014). *Genocide as social practice. Reorganizing society under Nazism and Argentina's military juntas*. Rutgers University Press. (Spanish original version: *El genocidio como práctica social: entre el nazismo y la experiencia argentina*, Buenos Aires, FCE, 2007)
Freud, S. (1953–1966). In J. Strachey, & A. Freud (Eds.), *The standard edition of the complete psychological works of Sigmund Freud* (24 vols.). The Hogarth Press and the Institute of Psycho-Analisis.
Freud, S. (1955) [1920]. Beyond the pleasure principle. In J. Strachey, & A. Freud (Eds.), *The standard edition of the complete psychological works of Sigmund Freud* (Vol. XVIII). The Hogarth Press and the Institute of Psycho-Analisis. 3–64.
Henniger, J. (2012). *The 99 Percent … of the Human Genome*. In *Science in the News*. Harvard Blogs. http://sitn.hms.harvard.edu/flash/2012/issue127a/
Kandel, E. R. (2007). *In search of memory: The emergence of a new science of mind*. W. W. Norton & Company.
Klein, N. (2007). *The Shock Doctrine: The rise of disaster capitalism*. Random House.
Laborit, H. (1983). *La colombe assassinée*. Grasset & Fasquelle.

Lashley, K. S. (1950). In search of the engram. In *Society for experimental biology, physiological mechanisms in animal behavior. (Society's symposium IV.)* (pp. 454–482). Academic Press.
Lehrer, J. (2007). *Proust was a neuroscientist.* Houghton Mifflin Harcourt.
Levinas, E. (1969). *Totality and infinity: An essay on exteriority* (A. Lingis, Trans.). Duquesne University Press.
Linton, M. (1975). Memory for real world events. In D. A. Norman, & D. E. Rumelhart (Eds.), *Explorations in cognition* (pp. 376–404). Freeman.
Linton, M. (1986). Ways of searching and the contents of memory. In D. C. Rubin (Ed.), *Autobiographical memory* (pp. 50–67). Cambridge University Press.
Nietzsche, F. (1989) [1886]. *Beyond good and evil.* Prometheus.
Piaget, P. (1977). *The grasp of consciousness: Action and concept in the young child.* Routledge.
Piaget, P. (1985). *The equilibration of cognitive structures: The Central problem of intellectual development.* University of Chicago Press.
Piaget, P., & García, R. (1989). *Psychogenesis and the history of science.* Columbia University Press.
Rose, S. (2006). *The 21st century brain. Explaining, mending and manipulating the mind.* Vintage Books.
Rosenfield, I. (1988). *The invention of memory. A new view of the brain.* Basic Books.
Rosenfield, I. (1992). *The strange, familiar and forgotten.* Alfred Knopf.
Rose, H., & Rose, S. (2016). *Can neuroscience change our minds?* Polity Press.
Sacks, O. (1997). *Un antropólogo en Marte. Siete historias paradójicas.* Norma.
Sacks, O. (2005). *El hombre que confundió a su mujer con un sombrero.* Anagrama.
Squire, L. R., Berg, D. K., Bloom, F. E., Lac, S., Ghosh, A., & Spitzer, N. C. (Eds.). (2012) *Fundamental neuroscience* (4th ed.). Academic Press.
Zeman, A. (2003). *Consciousness: A user's guide.* Yale University Press.
Zeman, A. (2006). What do we mean by "conscious" and "aware"? *Neuropsychological Rehabilitation, 16*(4), 356–376. https://doi.org/10.1080/09602010500484581

2
MEMORY, TRAUMA AND WORKING-THROUGH

Since its inception over a century ago, psychoanalysis has splintered into multiple schools of theory and technique. Today, not only are many of Freud's theories hotly disputed, but the effectiveness of psychoanalytic treatment is also questioned. Part of the problem lies in the lack of interdisciplinary dialogue mentioned in the "Introduction" of this book. As one distinguished psychoanalyst, Peter Fonagy, points out:

> There is little doubt that the absence of solid and persuasive evidence for the efficacy of psychoanalysis is the consequence of the self-imposed isolation of psychoanalysis from the empirical sciences.
>
> *(Fonagy, 2003, p. 74)*

Nevertheless, it is important to emphasize that these criticisms do not invalidate Freud's extraordinary intuitions about the nature of the unconscious. As Fonagy goes on to say:

> Recent reviews of neuroscientific work confirm that many of Freud's original observations, not least the pervasive influence of non-conscious processes and the organizing function of emotions for thinking, have found confirmation in laboratory studies.
>
> *(Fonagy, 2003, p. 75)*

With Fonagy's words in mind, this chapter will explore some of Sigmund Freud's ideas on memory – namely, representation, conscious and unconscious system, repression, trauma and working-through – together with those of more recent authors such as the French psychoanalyst René Kaës – in

DOI: 10.4324/9781003336464-3

particular, his notion of "pacts of denial" (Käes, 1976, 2007). In each case, the aim will be to provide a rich sociological analysis of the diverse consequences of massive state terror and to suggest ways to overcome its grim legacy.

Neuroscience relies on laboratory observations of how different neural networks are created, activated, deactivated and linked together. In contrast, psychoanalysis is based on clinical observations of behavioral disorders, such as phobias, obsessions and repetition compulsions, and patients' ability to reflect critically on these behaviors. In a more meta-reflective sense, our ability to uncover, reflect and evaluate can affect not only our actions (conscious or unconscious) but also our thoughts, desires, fears, dreams, obsessions, phobias, etc.

Neuroscience and psychoanalysis, then, start from different assumptions and construct knowledge in different ways. However, this does not mean that they are incompatible. Rather, they work on different levels of explanation. The explanations they provide for many of the phenomena that interest us here may still prove mutually enriching even if they are not reducible to each other. In order to avoid an overly eclectic approach, however, it is necessary to respect the accepted practices for data collection and analysis in each field – the way it approaches its objects of study and the types of argument and explanation it considers valid.

Freud revised his concept of "mental apparatus" several times over the years. Nevertheless, the notion of unconscious systems acting upon the information gathered by the perceptual apparatus is clearly related to what happens within the neural networks. Indeed, it is impossible to imagine a mental apparatus that is not based on neural connections, just as it is impossible to believe that neural networks operate directly on reality without being mediated by a mental structure. However, these two levels of analysis are of a different order: parallels can be found between them, but each has its own specificity and its own relatively precise limits.

In this chapter, I will examine more closely the relationship between memory processes and Freud's three systems of awareness: conscious system (Cs.), preconscious system (Pcs.) and unconscious system (Ucs.). This representation of the mental apparatus in terms of three *systems* is known in psychoanalysis as the "first topic." The "second topic" represents the mental apparatus in terms of three *agencies*: id, ego and superego. However, the latter move us away from neuronal networks toward symbolization processes, which are dealt with in Chapter 3 from the perspective of the social sciences.

Let us begin, then, with some preliminary questions that may help us map Freud's three systems onto the material substrate of neuronal networks:

- What would be recorded from lived experience in each of the three systems of the mental apparatus: conscious (Cs.), preconscious (Pcs.) and

unconscious (Ucs.)? At what levels and in what way would this record be laid down?
- What types of relations are established between these records and action, including a possible "inhibition" of action?
- How might psychoanalysis conceptualize the processes of "desensitization" described in the previous chapter, as well as the effects of these on psychic functioning, including emotional and cognitive capacities?
- How might different narratives change the way an experience is recorded in each one of the three systems (Cs., Pcs. and Ucs.)?
- And last but not least: What effects could such changes produce, both at the level of the action and of working-through?

Thing-representation and word-representation: Access to consciousness

One of Freud's greatest contributions to psychology is his account of the dynamic relations between the conscious and the unconscious mind – a topic that lies at the core of much of his work. Here we will focus on the types of representation that – so Freud believed – distinguishes each of these systems. Freud explored these ideas as early as 1900 in *The Interpretation of Dreams*, and developed it more fully in 1915 in his *Works on Metapsychology*, contrasting "thing-representations" with "word-representations." This distinction was to become the focus of his concerns in the 1920s, especially in two fundamental works, *Beyond the Pleasure Principle* and *Inhibitions, Symptoms and Anxiety* (Freud, 1953–1966).

In *The Unconscious*, Freud discusses the process of repression and the way representations might operate in both systems (Cs. and Ucs.), as well as the pathways joining them:

> If we communicate to a patient some idea which he has at one time repressed but which we have discovered in him, our telling him makes at first no change in his mental condition. Above all, it does not remove the repression nor undo its effects, as might perhaps be expected from the fact that the previously unconscious idea has now become conscious. On the contrary, all that we shall achieve at first will be a fresh rejection of the repressed idea. But now the patient has in actual fact the same idea in two forms in different places in his mental apparatus: first, he has the conscious memory of the auditory trace of the idea, conveyed in what we told him; and secondly, he also has – as we know for certain – the unconscious memory of his experience as it was in its earlier form. Actually, there is no lifting of the repression until the conscious idea, after the resistances have been overcome, has entered into connection with the unconscious memory-trace. It is only through the making conscious of the latter itself

that success is achieved. On superficial consideration this would seem to show that conscious and unconscious ideas are distinct registrations, topographically separated, of the same content. But a moment's reflection shows that the identity of the information given to the patient with his repressed memory is only apparent. To have heard something and to have experienced something are in their psychological nature two quite different things, even though the content of both is the same.

(Freud, 1953–1966, Volume XIV, pp. 175–176)

At this stage, it seems that Freud was still unable to decide between two alternative explanations for the relationship between conscious and unconscious representation. He was unsure whether a new transcription is made and stored elsewhere when a representation is made conscious or whether making a representation conscious simply changes its function.

Toward the end of *The Unconscious*, however, Freud proposed a third much more suggestive hypothesis: the conscious representation of an object consists of the word-representation and the thing-representation, the latter being a so-called cathexis of images of the thing (or similar things) in memory. Note that in Freud's theory the "id" is the origin of all psychic energy. Cathexis and anticathexis control how this energy is used or invested. Cathexis is the concentration of mental energy on one particular person, idea or object, while anticathexis (for example, repression) blocks cathexes or prevents them being used. Hypercathexis means an excessive cathexis.

What we have permissibly called the conscious presentation[1] of the object can now be split up into the presentation of the *word* and the presentation of the *thing*; the latter consists in the cathexis, if not of the direct memory-images of the thing, at least of remoter memory-traces derived from these.[2] We now seem to know all at once what the difference is between a conscious and an unconscious presentation [...]. The two are not, as we supposed, different registrations of the same content in different psychical localities, nor yet different functional states of cathexis in the same locality; but the conscious presentation comprises the presentation of the thing plus the presentation of the word belonging to it, while the unconscious presentation is the presentation of the thing alone. The [unconscious] system *Ucs.* contains the thing-cathexes of the objects, the first and true object-cathexes; the [pre-conscious] system *Pcs.* comes about by this thing-presentation being hypercathected through being linked with the word-presentations corresponding to it. It is these hypercathexes, we may suppose, that bring about a higher psychical organization and make it possible for the primary process to be succeeded by the secondary process which is dominant in the *Pcs*. Now, too, we are in a position to state precisely what it is that repression denies to the rejected presentation in the transference neuroses: what it denies to the presentation is translation into words which shall remain attached to the object. A presentation which is not put into words, or a psychical act which is not hypercathected, remains thereafter in the *Ucs.* in a state of repression.

(Freud, 1953–1966, Volume XIV, pp. 201–202)

Now, this hypothesis has several points in common with Gerald Edelman's theory presented in Chapter 1. Nevertheless, it is more complex despite the fact that it was formulated more than 60 years before Edelman's book of Neural Darwinism first appeared.

Freud states that the unconscious representation of the thing consists "if not of the direct memory-images of the thing, at least of remoter memory-traces derived from these." In other words, unconscious memories are scattered across different parts of the unconscious and only acquire meaning through words. At the biological level, Edelman imagined consciousness as a product of complex relationships of reentry between a set of subsystems united into a stable dynamic nucleus (Edelman & Tononi, 2000).

Both Freud and Edelman agree, then, that representations enter the mind through the unconscious system – especially long-term emotional memories, as studied by Kandel (see Chapter 1). But for Freud, it is language that allows what he describes as *hypercathexis*. It could be added that language endows an experience with a meaning that was not necessarily part of the original experience but is added by the subject after the event.

Freud also explains that it is not enough to give a meaning to an experience; this meaning must be *appropriate*. The subject must feel that what is communicated consciously corresponds to what was experienced unconsciously. Hence, the difficulty of working-through traumatic experiences. Working-through not only requires the *construction* of a narrative, but it requires the subject or subjects who have lived the experience to make this narrative their own.

As we will see later, this narrative is not constructed in isolation but through interactions with contemporaries and previous generations. For it is our predecessors who endow us and our world with meaning. In other words, meaning is *always* the product of social and historical processes and is linked to meanings sedimented within a society over time by earlier generations. We will return to these ideas in Chapter 3, which deals with philosophical, historical and the social science approaches to the problem of memory.

Edelman's idea that subsystems become integrated into a dynamic nucleus would seem to support Freud's second hypothesis, namely, that making an unconscious representation conscious involves a functional change. However, Freud's third hypothesis suggests that when unconscious representations are expressed in words and given meaning, they are not simply *integrated* but also *transformed*. This is actually more consistent with the epistemology on which neuroscience is founded than Edelman's own conclusions. To put it another way, Freud was more Edelmanian than Edelman himself. If neuroscience has failed to take Freud's ideas on board, it is mainly because of the suspicion and mutual misunderstanding that exist between two supposedly rival fields.

Freud's third hypothesis goes further. A "word-representation" has the potential to bring an experience or a memory trace into consciousness, but this does not necessarily occur. Hence, the distinction between the conscious and the preconscious system. The word-representation allows the representation to enter the preconscious system. From there it must follow another path to access consciousness. But this path is not straightforward or predetermined. Integrating unconscious contents into consciousness is always an idiosyncratic process. In Freud's own words:

> But word-presentations, for their part too, are derived from sense-perceptions, in the same way as thing-presentations are; the question might therefore be raised why presentations of objects cannot become conscious through the medium of their *own* perceptual residues. Probably, however, thought proceeds in systems so far remote from the original perceptual residues that they have no longer retained anything of the qualities of those residues, and, in order to become conscious, need to be reinforced by new qualities. Moreover, by being linked with words, cathexes can be provided with quality even when they represent only *relations* between presentations of objects and are thus unable to derive any quality from perceptions. Such relations, which become comprehensible only through words, form a major part of our thought-processes. As we can see, being linked with word-presentations is not yet the same thing as becoming conscious, but only makes it possible to become so; it is therefore characteristic of the [pre-conscious] system *Pcs.* and of that system alone.
>
> *(Freud, 1953–1966, Volume XIV, pp. 202–203)*

In other words, integrating unconscious material into consciousness is a creative act that assimilates lived experience into a web of meaning constructed together with other people, and allows us to process strong negative emotions. But people who have suffered trauma must feel that the new story is an authentic representation of their experience(s) in order to make it their own.

Leaving aside the differences between the three men, it is clear that Kandel, Edelman and Freud put forward hypotheses that go to the heart of this book. They all suggest that memory processes are creators of meaning. By putting experience into words and narrative forms of expression, they seek to give a coherent structure to past experiences in the present, a social appropriation of the past in order to transform present actions.

Drives and their destinations: The origin of the mechanism of repression

Let us now turn to Freud's analysis of the system of drives and the role played in it by repression. Unfortunately, James Strachey, the general editor of *The Standard Edition of the Complete Psychological Works of Sigmund Freud*, chose to translate Freud's "Trieb" (motivational drive) as "instinct" and "Trieblehre" (theory of motivational drives) as "theory of instincts."[3] This has given rise to the mistaken idea that drives are purely biological, are triggered by specific stimuli, and always follow an identical pattern (Kirsch & Mertens, 2018). Similarly, Strachey uses the term "instinctual impulses" to translate "Triebregungen," which in fact refers to specific "activations" or manifestations of a drive. It should be remembered, then, that what is repressed is not an instinct or even the drive itself but an ideational presentation of the drive.

In fact, Freud includes repression among four defenses against anxiety-producing "instinctual impulses." He classifies these in terms of the "destination of drive," that is, the direction in which unconscious energy is redirected. In addition to repression, these mechanisms include "reversal into the opposite" (for example, showing love toward people we really hate), "turning around on the self (the clearest example of which is turning sadism into masochism) and sublimation (for example, when a sadist becomes a surgeon).

This work will not address the complex debates both inside and outside of psychoanalysis surrounding Freud's theory of drives. However, it is worth commenting on the connection that Freud makes between stimuli and action. This will clarify both the functional nature of repression and some of the behavior associated with it, particularly "repetition compulsion."

In developing the concept of drive from physiology, Freud maintains that

> a stimulus applied from the outer world to living tissue (nervous substance) is discharged by action. The action answers the purpose of withdrawing the substance affected from the operation of the stimulus, removing it out of range of the stimulus.
>
> *(Freud, 2008, p. 72)*

But Freud distinguishes between physiological stimuli (those that depend on the outside world, like light hurting the eye) and stimuli which come from within the body itself, such as dryness in the throat or acidity in the stomach lining and which are ultimately caused by "instinctual impulses."[4]

The fundamental difference between external stimuli and internal "instinctual impulses" is that external stimuli exert a *momentary* force (even if this can be repeated indefinitely), while the force exerted by "instinctual impulses" is constant. The fact that impulses are internal and constant prevents the subject from implementing the classic defenses against stimuli (fight or flight). Instead, the impulse becomes a need which is balanced by being "satisfied." This idea of "equilibration" can be linked to the work of genetic psychology, especially Piaget (1985).

Freud first presented the idea that the mind seeks pleasure and avoids pain in his *Project for a Scientific Psychology* of 1895, in which he also theorized about the possibility of representing memory at the synaptic level. Later, he hypothesized that an increase in external stimuli or internal impulses led to an increase in "unpleasure" while a decrease led to "pleasure." However, Freud himself recognized that the mechanism of repression is not easy to deduce from his own theory:

> It is not easy in theory to deduce the possibility of such a thing as repression. Why should an instinctual impulse undergo a vicissitude like this? A necessary condition of its happening must clearly be that the instinct's attainment of its aim should produce unpleasure instead of pleasure. But we cannot well imagine such a contingency. There are no such instincts: satisfaction of an instinct is always pleasurable. We should have to assume certain peculiar circumstances, some sort of process by which the pleasure of satisfaction is changed into unpleasure.
> *(Freud, 1953–1966, Volume XIV, p. 146)*

The solution to this problem, Freud claimed, was that satisfying the repressed impulse might do more harm than good:

> the satisfaction of an instinct which is under repression would be quite possible, and further, that in every instance such a satisfaction would be pleasurable in itself; but it would be irreconcilable with other claims and intentions. It would, therefore, cause pleasure in one place and unpleasure in another. It has consequently become a condition for repression that the motive force of unpleasure shall have acquired more strength than the pleasure obtained from satisfaction.
> *(Freud, 1953–1966, Volume XIV, p. 147)*

He adds that repression is only possible once a person's psyche has become sharply divided into conscious and unconscious:

> before the mental organization reaches this stage, the task of fending off instinctual impulses is dealt with by the other vicissitudes which instincts may undergo – e.g. reversal into the opposite or turning round upon the subject's own self.
> *(Freud, 1953–1966, Volume XIV, p. 147)*

Freud distinguishes two stages of repression. The first stage consists of excluding an idea or ideational event from consciousness. This "primal" or "primary" repression establishes a nucleus that attracts associations or related trains of thought in a second stage that Freud calls "proper" or "secondary" repression. Freud considers that repression would probably fail if these two forces – conscious repression and unconscious attraction – did not cooperate.

But Freud claims that what is repressed does not disappear completely. All repression, as a rule, create a "substitutive formation" that allows the repressed element to return to conscious life and to behavior. The repressed content is displaced onto something less threatening or painful. A classic example of dream-distortion is the Wolf Man's dream replacing his need to be loved by his father; but the same mechanism produces *behavior* through phobias, hysterias, obsessions as well as giving rise to failures, blockages, forgetfulness and jokes. In the latter, the person "does not remember anything of what he [sic] has forgotten and repressed, but acts it out. He reproduces it not as a memory but as an action; he repeats it, without of course knowing that he is repeating it" (Freud, 1953–1966, Volume XII, p. 150).

One such behavior is of central importance in this chapter: *repetition-compulsion*. Even if what is repeated is not necessarily the original experience, *repetition-compulsion* allows what is repressed in the unconscious and cannot be remembered to be acted out in various complex ways. In later life, Freud believed that the compulsion to repeat was more primitive and instinctual than the pleasure principle, existing even in matter itself. The notion of *repetition-compulsion* as a prototypical behavioral manifestation of repression is enormously useful for understanding memory processes. So far, neither the social sciences nor philosophy has paid it sufficient attention.

Let us turn now to the "the traumatic," a topic that brings us closer to the purpose of this chapter. The concept of trauma has been widely discussed, not only in connection with Freud but also with later thinkers. Many of these discussions have proved enlightening, but others have trivialized the notion beyond recognition. I will now review these discussions before looking at the consequences of repetition-compulsion and one of its most important intersubjective manifestations: *denegative pacts* or *pacts of denial*.

The traumatic

In *Beyond the Pleasure Principle*, Freud defines the traumatic as:

> Such external excitations as are strong enough to break through the barrier against stimuli. In my opinion the concept of trauma involves such a relationship to an otherwise efficacious barrier.
> *(Freud, 1953–1966, Volume XVIII, p. 34)*

This definition is useful for understanding how trauma overwhelms the day-to-day functioning of the ego, insofar as it cannot be integrated into a coherent narrative of the self. Indeed, Laplanche and Pontalis, authors of the influential *Dictionary of Psychoanalysis* (1988), define trauma as "an event in the subject's life defined by its intensity, by the subject's incapacity to respond to it adequately, the inability of individuals to respond to it properly and by the upheaval and long-lasting effects it brings about in the psychical organization" (Laplanche & Pontalis, 1988, p. 465).

These are by no means the only definitions, but they are perhaps the most used and cited.

The question asked by many of Freud's successors is how trauma leaves marks in the mental apparatus? what kind of marks these could be? and, above all, how they impact on subsequent actions? These questions have led to numerous theories, ranging from those of Freud's contemporaries, Sandor Ferenczi or Morton Prince, through those of William Brown and William Sargant, who treated shell-shocked soldiers during World War I and II, respectively, to the modern psychiatric concept of post-traumatic stress disorder (PTSD), which was partly developed to treat delayed stress reactions in U.S. veterans of the Korean and Vietnam wars.[5] Similarly, numerous studies of trauma among Nazi concentration camp survivors have been published, and there are some studies of survivors of Latin American dictatorships (Danieli, 1998; Kordon et al., 2012; Puget & Käes, 1991). These are just part of a flood of works drawing on structuralism, literary theory and post-modernism, among other approaches, that are constantly broadening the concept of trauma and creating expressions such as "collective trauma," which is quite debatable (i.e. Robben, 2008).

One influential answer to the question of how trauma affects psychic organization has come from neuroscience (Van der Kolk, 1998; Van der Kolk et al., 1984) and literary criticism (Caruth, 1995, 1996). They recognize that it is in the very nature of traumatic memory to be dissociated, and to be initially stored as sensory fragments that have no linguistic components. They both argue that these fragments must be stored in a specific system for recording traumatic events, rather than being processed on a symbolic level like ordinary information. In this sense, traumatic memories are "true" records of experience registered "as it was" without any interpretation. This is not an argument that I support in this book. However, given its widespread acceptance in the Anglo-Saxon world, in both neuroscience and literary studies, I would like to explain briefly why I do not agree with the idea of a separate memory system for traumatic experiences.

Van der Kolk's work on trauma is based on his studies of nightmares among American soldiers returning from Vietnam. He concludes that these patients' nightmares differ significantly from the nightmares of non-traumatized people because they take place at different times in the sleep cycle. Van der Kolk claims that these trauma-related dreams are a literal restaging of the traumatic event (Van der Kolk et al., 1984).

In line with poststructuralist literary or cultural theory, Caruth, on the other hand, takes Freud's notion of the unconscious to mean that the domain of trauma is "unrepresentable." She finds support in Van der Volk's work for her claim that trauma somehow imprints itself "literally" on the victim's mind in such a way that it cannot be symbolized (Caruth, 1995, 1996).

Ruth Leys has criticized the notion of the "unspeakable" and the "unrepresentable" in no uncertain terms (Leys, 2000). She highlights the failure of Van der Kolk and his team to use control groups in most of their studies of American soldiers, and the inappropriate comparisons they make in the few cases where they do use control groups. She criticizes their "forced" interpretations that do not follow logically from the experiments themselves, and that present conjectures as findings. Moreover, she shows that these findings directly contradict those of similar research on sleep and the inscription of traumatic memory. In fact, the only serious criticism that Leys does not make is that Van der Kolk and his team offer no evidence that traumatic memories are any different from other emotional memories (see Lansky & Bley, 1995; Hartmann, 1996; Masling, 1960 to support it). This is despite the fact that as neuroscientists they must be aware of Eric Kandel's work discussed in Chapter 1.

In the case of Caruth, Leys points out her use of incomplete and edited quotations designed to put words into Freud's mouth. Caruth makes him say what she wants to demonstrate – the "literalness" of the traumatic inscription, the traumatic as "departure"– as elements of literary theory that are not found as such in Freud's work, but are introduced by Caruth herself, rewriting the father of psychoanalysis from her own perspective.

But while Leys confronts these perspectives head on, she fails to offer an alternative explanation. Moreover, she appears skeptical and distrustful of the very concept of trauma, and calls for an "intelligent, humane and human pragmatism" to confront what she calls Caruth's "totalizing" approach to human suffering. This skepticism also runs through another body of work on memory, some of it is produced at the Kulturwissenschaftliches Institut in Essen, by Harald Welzer and Christian Gudehus's teams (Gudehus et al., 2010).

At the risk of venturing into a difficult field, there are alternatives to either abandoning the concept of trauma completely or accepting – as Caruth and Van der Kolk do – that trauma is recorded "literally" in the unconscious. For example, it is plausible that what is registered intact is the affect produced by the traumatic experience: feelings of terror, impotence and annihilation of the self, and not the actual experience. Experiences, as neuroscience shows, are stored across numerous fragmented memory systems, and there is no reason to suppose that traumatic experiences are treated any differently. What we are talking about here would be a preliminary recording of the experience. Later we will consider whether this non-narrative recording is a first *symbolization* of the experience, one that is unable to become a word-representation or narrative due to the threat it poses to the person's sense of identity.

Far from being imprinted on some supposedly special system for traumatic memories (Van der Kolk's thesis), then, it would seem that a preliminary recording of the experience does take place but that this recording remains locked in the unconscious because of the threat it poses to the individual's on-going sense of identity. It cannot be integrated as a "representation." Instead, it continues to exert an indirect effect on the other subsystems, without going through the mediation and control of the conscious system, as described in the previous chapter.

Nicolas Abraham and Maria Torok have classified different types of symbolization produced by the mental apparatus. In their view, this preliminary recording of the traumatic experience is also a first level of symbolization (Abraham & Torok, 2005). Without entering into the discussion about which levels of symbolization would become effective in a traumatic situation, what can be observed is that these first levels of symbolization do not manage to transform themselves into "word-representations," much less organize themselves into a discourse. This does not detract from the fact that "thing-representations" are also a level of "representation" and not a literal inscription, while the transformation of the stimulus into a "thing-representation" already implies (as its name indicates) a level of representation and, therefore, perhaps the possibility of a certain non-narrative symbolization.

It is likely, then, that when verbalizing the trauma presents a possible risk, this blocks its access to consciousness. The emotion is there – and it could even be symbolized as a feeling – but, since it is inaccessible, it cannot be processed. Therefore, it continues unaltered. But what remains unaltered is not the experience itself, but the feeling or emotion generated in the individual by this experience.

Because this feeling cannot be integrated into an episodic narrative structure, it dislocates the individual's narrative identity. In the case of the social and historical traumas produced by the experience of State violence in Latin America, René Kaës maintains:

> Just as the first thing torturers always do is to break the fundamental temporal rhythms of life, the first act of catastrophic social violence is to establish terror by dismantling thought processes. That is why the abolition of the symbolic order gives the maddening status of a phantasmal representation in the psyche to the object that has disappeared. The anxiety

aroused by terror cannot be cannot be repressed or projected, or linked to representations of things and words, things and words, or find representations and objects in linguistic and social symbols.

(Puget & Käes, 1991, p. 167)

Käes's example introduces another key element into the equation, and not only because it refers specifically to state violence. From a more general theoretical perspective, *trauma is produced and renewed as a social and historical experience*. The subject does not live or experience any traumatic situation in isolation; both the experience and the feeling it produces happen within the context of meaningful relationships with others. The shame, pain and terror are felt in relation to other people, whether these are external or internalized in what Freud called the *superego*.

The works of Argentine Team of Psychosocial Work and Investigation (EATIP) define this question quite precisely:

We consider that the term "psychic imprint" refers to the point where trauma (as an event whose intensity and quality is potentially pathological, depending on the subject's psychic

development and defence mechanisms) meshes with the subject's narcissistic sense of self (which involves the past history of the subject's personal identity formation and interactions with significant others).

(CINTRAS et al., 2009, p. 162)

They go on to say:

The issue of trauma is linked not only to the degree of destructuring caused by the stimulus, but also the meaning the stimulus acquires for each person, and his or her ability to find or maintain adequate support for the psyche. But both the individual meaning of trauma and the ability to maintain or obtain adequate support are linked in these cases to the social understandings of the traumatic situation. And, of course, these are linked to the subject's complemental series. The traumatic effect occurs because there is still a residue of unsymbolized anxiety.

(CINTRAS et al., 2009, p. 163)

In short, trauma is experienced and can be understood only within a social context. It will remain "activated" in the present for as long as conditions exist that made the feeling traumatic. The antidote to this situation is to make the trauma conscious through a process that Freud described in German as *Durcharbeiten* (working-through).

One theorist who has used a mainly sociological perspective to examine the relationship between the individual and the social in creating and perpetuating trauma is Dominick LaCapra. This is how he summarizes this perspective and compares Freud's "individual" approach with collective approaches to repression, memory and working-through:

> I believe that this concern, both in Freud and in others [i.e. analogy between the individual and the social] is based on mistaken individualistic ideological assumptions and gives rise to misguided questions. One should rather call into question the very idea that one is working with a more or less flimsy analogy between the individual and society and argue instead that there is nothing intrinsically "individual" about such concepts as repression and working-through. These concepts refer to processes that always involve modes of interaction, mutual reinforcement, conflict, censorship, orientation towards others, and so forth, and their relatively individual or collective status should not be prejudged.
>
> *(LaCapra, 1998, p. 43)*

This means that memory processes clearly occur within the mental apparatus of one or more subjects and not within social groups – hence the problematic nature of concepts such as "social trauma" or "collective trauma." Nevertheless, they are linked in various complex ways to historical and social factors either in the past, where the trauma occurred, or in the present, where it continues, or both. And social influences are both direct (real interactions with significant others) and indirect (symbolic interactions with internalized others) (Käes et al., 1996).

In short, it could be said that trauma originates in a historical and social situation (historical in terms of time and social in terms of interactions with others) and its consequences are manifested in the individual psyche. These consequences are incompatible with a coherent sense of identity and for this reason the creation of subjectively understandable meanings in the form of "word-representations" is blocked. A reified form, perhaps even a non-narrative symbolization of the experience, becomes anchored in the unconscious system and it is here that the mechanism of repression operates.

This sensation – or set of sensations – not transformed into words, is manifested through action in endless ways and is activated by numerous situations, also historical and social. These trigger behaviors that are harmful or problematic for the individuals concerned and for their environment. Such behaviors include phobias, hysteria and compulsions. At the same time, when these come from primordial repression – that is, a psychic fixation on an inner "object" –, they tend to produce a compulsion to repeat situations similar to that experienced as traumatic. This *repetition compulsion* may lead to individuals adopting the same or different roles in a series of different but comparable situations.

Desensitization, repetition and pacts of denial

The consequences of the traumatic situation can be expressed at various levels. On the one hand, the process of denial may take the form of repetition. Freud describes this clearly in *Inhibitions, Symptoms and Anxiety*:

> The two techniques I refer to are undoing what has been done (*ungeschehenmachen*) and isolating (*isolieren*) back very far. It is, as it were, a negative magic, and endeavours, by means of motor symbolism, to 'blow away' not merely the consequence of some occurrence, experience or impression, but those very events themselves, [...] This endeavour to undo shades off into normal behavior in the case in which a person decides to regard an event as not having happened. But whereas he will take no direct steps against the event, and will simply look away from it and its consequences, the neurotic person will try to make the past itself non-existent. He will try to repress it by motor means. The same aim may perhaps be present in and account for the compulsion to repeat actions which is so frequently met with in obsessional neuroses and which serves a number of contradictory purposes at once. When anything has not happened in the desired way it can be undone by being repeated in a different way; and now all the motives that exist for lingering over such repetitions come into play as well.
>
> (Freud, 1936, pp. 72–74)

At the social level, *repetition compulsion* is related to a transubjective phenomenon that several authors have called the *denegative pact* (or pact of denial), that is, an unconscious agreement not to mention the traumatic event. It is a way of socializing what Freud called "efforts to hunt," characterized as a persecution not only of the repressed scene – which is inaccessible to consciousness – but any offshoot of it, any element that could produce some association.

René Kaës describes how the denegative pact works:

> The denegative pact also plays a part in transubjective or group repression memory formation; its unspoken formula could be: do not remember that which could endanger our relationship, which is more precious than the memory of what happened, because what happened has already happened to us all. In this context, the denegative pact maintains the narcissistic contract and contributes to the formation of shared screen memories and myths, [the latter being] the screen memories of [whole] peoples. The denegative pact is also a part of the repetition through which catastrophic experiences and traumas are expressed. Couples, families, groups, institutions and societies each have their own kind of repetition mechanisms.

Consequently, each manages the psychic repetitions at their own particular level and preserves them.

(Puget & Käes, 1991, p. 177)

The *denegative pact* is part of the logic of repetition, yet it establishes an unspoken consensus to favor more repression. This operates by extending what cannot and should not be said to the whole community and by silencing those who attempt to speak out. Trauma operates on individual subjectivity, destroying any vestige of self-confidence that those involved in the pact may have retained previously and preventing them from appropriating their own history. The pact alienates individuals not only from their own experience but also from any narrative account of the traumatic event. They remain detached and unable to relate such stories to their *own experience*.

In Chapter 4, we will see how various discourses on socio-historical events of massive state violence in Latin America combine with these *denegative pacts* to produce collective mechanisms of alienation and distancing. This is achieved through narratives that deliberately exclude the first person and recount these events as something that happened *to others*. This is not a conspiracy or even conscious process. Narratives emerge and gain hegemony as they become enmeshed with denegative pacts, and that is the reason for their success.

Finally, trauma produces a desensitization that, like repression, operates at the individual and subjective level but also has cumulative social and historical effects. One way to face a traumatic event that has broken through what Freud calls our "anti-stimulus protection" is to disguise the loss of feeling behind a general desensitization. This is done by disconnecting the mental apparatus from most of the sensations produced by the environment. As we saw in the previous chapter, this is an adaptive response – a reaction to a pain that cannot be either avoided or confronted.

When it refers to events that affect large population groups, this cumulative desensitization is expressed in social and historical terms as a self-reinforcing ideology. This ideology hinges on the *lack of meaning* that results from the (alleged) impossibility of understanding the traumatic event. Here, a deliberate and ideologically justified refusal to seek one's own identity will be called the *ideology of nonsense*.

This ideology may be accompanied by cynicism or, less frequently, by nihilism, satire or ridicule.

From this point of view, the *ideology of nonsense* is a *more advanced stage of repression*, an attempt to create meaning. Far from challenging the denegative pact, it seeks to voice it at a conscious level. By giving the pact a narrative solidity, it seeks to restore some sort of coherent identity. Ironically, it does so by denying the very existence of the self that was previously destroyed.

As Edelman points out, the sensation of absence is less tolerable than the absence of sensation. Thus, just as body image is adjusted to compensate for the lack of a limb, so the *ideology of nonsense* restores coherence by pretending one's own identity never existed. A meaningless past is perpetuated in a meaningless present.

In the next chapter, we will see how Bergson describes absence and the void left by absence. We will see how something only disappears definitively when this void is filled with something else, in this case *nonsense stories* that attempt to hide the loss and close off the mourning process (although in fact they make the latter impossible).

Working-through

One of the clearest definitions of the concept of *Durcharbeiten* can be found in *Inhibitions, symptoms and anxiety*, where Freud states

> For we find that even after the ego has decided to relinquish its resistances it still has difficulty in undoing the repressions; and we have called the period of strenuous effort which follows after its praiseworthy decision, the phase of 'working through'. The dynamic factor which makes a working through of this kind necessary and comprehensible is not far to seek. It must be that after the ego resistance has been removed the power of the repetition – compulsion – the attraction exerted by the unconscious prototypes upon the repressed instinctual process – has yet to be overcome. This factor might well be described as the resistance of the unconscious.
> *(Freud, 1936, p. 148)*

Dominick LaCapra also provides an interesting definition for this term when he suggests:

> Working-through would thus seem to involve a modified mode of repetition offering a measure of critical purchase on problems and responsible control in action that would allow a desirable change. It is thus intimately bound up with the possibility of ethically responsible action and critical judgement on the part of someone who strives for the position of an agent and may thereby counteract his or her own experience of victimhood and the incapacitating effects of trauma.
> *(LaCapra, 1998, p. 186)*

Working-through is thus an attempt to act in a critical and ethically responsible manner, in order to create or reconstruct a sense of meaning. It seeks to overcome unconscious resistances – in as much as this is possible – including repetition compulsion.

Like sublimation, *working-through* belongs to a group of Freudian concepts that lack theoretical development but, nevertheless, occupy a central place in the psychoanalytic literature. Freud himself considered that *working-through* is what distinguishes psychoanalysis from other talking cures. It is what makes psychoanalysis original as a clinical treatment and different from other types of psychotherapy.

However, as has already been argued in relation to trauma, it is not possible to think about working-through except as a process that occurs in a relationship with other people. This point is very important. It is the other – a psychoanalyst, a relative or close friend with whom we have shared life experiences, perhaps even a child – who challenges us to question our traumatic repetitions of repressed historical content. Working-through is, in itself, a historical and social process.

Thus, the idea of *social processes of recovery from trauma* is not simply an attempt to transfer – by analogy – the concept of working-through from the individual to the trans-subjective or even the social level. It is based on a more radical assumption, namely, that the changes brought about by trauma always occur at the level of inter-subjective links or bonds.

However, not all meanings are reconstructed in these processes of working-through. As mentioned earlier, some forms of meaning-creation restore a certain coherence – but only at the cost of legitimizing denegative pacts. These pacts are based on the very denial of the subject's previous identity. In other words, the pact states that there has not been any destruction of identity because there was nothing to destroy in the first place.

Another more subtle way in which this denial of identity destruction operates is through a concept that is in vogue today: *resilience*. Ana Berezin and Gilou García Reinoso have lucidly described its paradoxes and contradictions:

> The concept and practice of resilience comes in direct line with behaviorism, starting from a banal observation, an obvious observable fact: not everyone reacts in the same way or records impacts of the same magnitude to stressful events or even to those of a traumatic nature. In line with the notion of "human engineering" and a phenomenon observed in physics, the resilience applied to the human being, it is argued that subjects capable of withstanding great stress can learn from adversity. Thus educators or psychologists or social workers should apply this notion to everyone who has suffered a trauma. In other words, these subjects reconstruct themselves after a breakdown, catastrophe or destructive violence and become stronger without any traumatic damage remaining.
>
> *(Berezin & García Reinoso, 2010, pp. 60–61)*

And they continue their criticism by stating that

> With resilience, a practice for survival, a value concept is invented and a practice is proposed that tends to reinforce it. Instead of working so that some human truth can emerge and transform the conditions of life, and not simply make them bearable [...] those who are dedicated to deploying a practice and a theory (rather an ideology) of resilience run the risk of promoting an adaptation to the suffering produced by violence, hunger and exclusion in which our societies and many of their inhabitants [sic] live or survive.
>
> *(Berezin & García Reinoso, 2010, p. 63)*

The discourse of resilience is thus another way of blocking the mourning process. Even though it does not deny the self's previous existence, it accepts the self's destruction and the individual's ability to bear this as something normal.

We cannot be absolutely certain about which meanings would help in the working-though process and which would simply reinforce the repressive and/or negative cycle. However, it is certainly more enriching to attempt to understand things from the other end of the relationship, as Berezin and García Reinoso do, by analyzing *the present consequences of different attempts to give meaning to past experience*. Such an analysis would allow us to evaluate their potential for working-through, which would always take place inter-subjectively within a historical and social context. The *effectiveness for working-through* of different sorts of meaning creation can be observed in a person's daily behavior, and it is here that we must look.

However, it is fundamental to emphasize that *working-through* and *acting out* are not polar opposites. Working-through facilitates understanding but in many cases it reduces rather than completely eliminating the compulsion to act out. At the same time, acting out does not necessarily exclude the possibility of reconstructing the meaning of a trauma, at least partially. The reality of the mind – like many other realities – is too complex for us to understand completely. And some psychoanalytical approaches have at times tended to oversimplify and trivialize the complexity of Freudian thought.[6]

Although this may seem discouraging given the enormous work it requires, working-through cannot produce a complete *cure* in the sense of removing all the symptoms or anguish produced by the trauma. What it can do is alleviate or reduce *some* of its effects based on an understanding of how repression works and of *some* of the effects of the past on our present.

It is true that given our contemporary thirst for complete and exhaustive knowledge, this definition of working-through may seem insipid. But at the same time, it constitutes an immeasurably qualitative difference with the past. It offers the wonderful possibility of encountering, or to be more precise, re-encountering ourselves in the first person of the plural. It is a way to begin processing our grief and sorrow without *ceasing to be who we are*, without giving up on the process of constructing and reconstructing our identity after terror, and without naturalizing the destruction of social relations.

Working-through as a social and historical process

If working-through trauma is a social and historical process, then it occurs most emphatically in the area of power relations. It is linked to the struggle to re-establish a greater level of self-determination, bearing in mind the sense of original Greek word *autonomia*, from *autonomos* "having its own laws."

By working – with others – to recover and resignify our repressed past, we seek to make ourselves ethically responsible for the past, present and future consequences of our actions, and to locate and confront or contain the impulses that give rise to them. That is precisely what the "malaise in culture" described by Freud is about, culture as a process of social and historical working-through that allows us to use the past – even a traumatic one – as a warning and an ethical constraint on human activity

Both state terror and the ideology of nonsense that normally follows it in survivor societies create resistance to the ethical and political assumptions that underpin working-through. Both processes are interrelated and seek to break the relationship between past and present that allows us to keep our behavior morally in check.

A major outcome of trauma following systematic terror is the destruction of identity together with a breakdown of self-confidence and, consequently, of confidence in others. Terror seeks to break the self by forcing it to do what it knows it *cannot* and *should not* do. This has been the rationale of torture since the late Middle Ages, when it was first used by the Inquisition as part of the embryonic technology of genocidal power.

Torture would be unnecessary if the goal were only to defeat or disarm the enemy. That is why not every war or defeat is necessarily traumatic. Torture sets out to achieve more than the destruction of the will to fight. It seeks the surrender of the victims' identity by forcing them to say or do things they should not say or do, such as denying their religious, national, political or sexual convictions, providing information that will harm loved ones, or giving their affection or sexuality to a person that they find repugnant.

Similarly, the concentration camp system seeks to break the inmates' will through a procedure as terrifying as torture itself: the threat of torture. The extreme pain of torture has proven to be quite effective in destroying a person's identity. But, from the Inquisition to the present day, the fear of torture has been a much more effective tool, insofar as terror of the unknown generates a level of anguish and uncertainty much greater than any pain, however extreme. It is very difficult for the mind to prepare itself to face a stimulus that it does not know, especially when the classic responses (confrontation or escape) are impossible.

The *ideology of nonsense* is really an attempt to preserve the self through desensitization in the face of traumatic terror. However, by resorting to desensitization and the negative pact to give meaning to unconscious horrors, the narrative ends up legitimizing and justifying the earlier destruction of the self. Far from working-through terror, it simply makes the destruction of the self invisible.

The *ideology of nonsense* not only makes it impossible to recognize the harm done by the destruction of the self. It makes it impossible to talk about this destruction. This is not simply the silence of repression. Working-through has been replaced by *a different narrative*, one that maintains that there is no identity to recover and nothing to heal because, in truth, there was never anything there to begin with. The experiences of terror, torture and trauma themselves are not denied – what is denied is the identity that these destroyed. Thus, *nonsense* becomes a dogmatic and circular story which allows the repressed sensation to be given a narrative outlet.

The logic of nonsense, then, should not be confused with working-through in the Freudian sense of *Durcharbeiten*. Rather, it is a kind of *word-representation* of the process of *repression* itself, a further – historical and social step toward demolishing identity. As such, it follows the same logic as I have described in previous works as the "symbolic enactment of genocidal social practices" (Feierstein, 2014).

The symbolic enactment of genocide refers to the process whereby society comes to accept that identity, self, social relations and protest movements have not only vanished but never really existed. Thus, there is no self to be reconstructed and no working-through to be done, because there was never really a self or a subject to be destroyed – only nothingness, inert matter scattered randomly about the universe, disguised with masks that can be peeled away like the layers of an onion.

Philosophically, this ideology is structured around the conviction that nothing exists behind these masks, that there is no one behind the characters that are represented. And if life itself is meaningless, then we can reconcile ourselves more easily with the idea that *our own lives* have no meaning either.

Marcelo Viñar is one of the authors who has most clearly identified the psychosocial consequences of terror:

> In previous works we insisted that the experience of torture cannot be reduced to the repertoire of violence and physical and psychological aggression. These are only means or instruments of a lucid and well-articulated system that aims to destroy the beliefs of the victims and to strip them of the relationship with themselves, their ideals and their memory.
>
> *(Viñar in Puget & Käes, 1991, pp. 64–65)*

58 Memory, trauma and working-through

For this reason, Viñar considers psychoanalysis to be an ideal method and setting for "attempting the adventure of symbolizing the deadly heritage we inherited from the black decade, and working through it to make it communicable.[7] Fighting oblivion and revenge, engraving a memory, and punishing crime by constructing a history" (Viñar in Puget & Käes, 1991, pp. 64–65).

If the processes described here – memory construction and working-through as well as *denial* – are social and historical in nature, then politicians, academics, intellectuals and judges also create tools for working-through or for denial in representations they construct of the past. LaCapra recognized this clearly and crudely, even though those who cite him usually pay little attention to this point:

> To have a social role, it must be articulated with political concerns. Addressing such concerns requires a combination of the roles or subjective positions of scholar and critical intellectual, a combination that does not dispense with rigorous scholarship or conflate critical reflection with partisan propaganda but does render allowable and even desirable modes of thought that often are discouraged in academy.
> *(LaCapra, 1998, p. 205)*

It is not a question of demanding that judges, academics, psychologists or politicians abandon a critical approach and adopt the "discourse of working through." Even if such a thing could be formulated, its dogmatic nature would be truly absurd, useless and even comical.

On the contrary, it would to fail to understand LaCapra's injunction that it is necessary to abandon the positivist illusion and take responsibility for the consequences of one's own actions, judgments, analysis and reflections, at least as they appear at a certain place and time. In our particular case, it means taking responsibility for the effects of political, legal, intellectual, judicial, psychoanalytic or academic work insofar as they may contribute to working-through trauma or, alternatively, (re)producing denial, repetitions and desensitization.

Freud, quoting a well-known poem, once stated that "The benighted traveller may sing aloud in the dark to deny his own fears; but, for all that, he will not see an inch further beyond his nose" (Freud, 1936, p. 96). It seems that it is not enough to replace the mark of trauma with words, at least not just any words. It is a question, then, of asking oneself what these words allow and make possible, and of making ourselves responsible for their effects, if only the effects that we are capable of distinguishing, supposing or imagining.

Notes

1 Original footnote from the Standard Edition: "*Vorstellung.*" This word has as a rule been translated above by "idea" (see Footnote 1, p. 174.). From this point till the end of the chapter, "*Vorstellung*" is uniformly translated by "*presentation*" –

"*Wortvorstellung*" "presentation of the word" or "word-presentation"; "*Sachvorstellung*" "presentation of the thing" or "thing-presentation." These words were formerly translated by the somewhat misleading "verbal idea" and "concrete idea." In "Mourning and Melancholia" (below, p. 256), Freud replaced "*Sachvorstellung*" by the synonymous "*Dingvorstellung*"; and he had used this second version earlier, in *The Interpretation of Dreams (1900a), Standard Ed.*, 4, 295–296, and near the beginning of Chapter 4 of his book on Jokes (1905c).
2 Here, Freud uses the term *Sachvorstellung*, which is translated in the Standard Edition as *presentation of the thing*. In other works, Freud also uses *Dingvorstellung*, even though in German, *Sache* and *Ding* are not synonymous, since the former refers to the thing understood in its material sense and the latter to the thing in the abstract sense. Freud first used the term thing-presentation – in contrast to word-presentation – in his early paper on aphasia. Unlike his contemporaries, Freud proposed an understanding of language in which memories and ideas were not located in specific parts of the brain. Thing-presentation (or object-presentation as he originally called it) stood for an olfactory, kinaesthetic or visual impression of a thing in the real world.
3 Lacan objected strongly to "the translation of instinct for Trieb [drive] ... thus basing the whole edition on a complete misunderstanding since Trieb and instinct have nothing in common." (Lacan, 1994, p. 49)
4 It is worth noting that it is Freud's early view of drive stimuli linked to self-preservation that has been prioritized here, without entering into an analysis of sexual drives. The whole theory of drives, and in particular of the discharge system, has been quite lucidly questioned by John Bowlby, in his trilogy *Attachment and Loss* (Bowlby, 1973), among other authors and replaced by a more complex system linked to the search for homeostasis. But this discussion is clearly outside the scope of the present work. In any case, all psychoanalytic writers agree on the interpretation of the Freudian concepts used in this chapter, irrespective of their differences with respect to the possible consequences or derivations of this analysis.
5 The concept of "post-traumatic stress" is strongly questioned by many authors as a way of pathologizing the social, political and subjective experience of trauma.
6 In the everyday language and practice of psychoanalysis – at least in Argentina, a country of psychoanalysts and psychoanalyzed individuals par excellence – the clinical terminology from the field of medical practice has become established, with expressions such as "discharge," which would involve the confirmation of a healing process. It is difficult, from the Freudian point of view, to believe that a subject can function in such a way as to abolish the mechanism of repression and that the process of working-through lead to fully conscious behavior. Such a psychoanalytic utopia would undoubtedly create a subject whom we do not know, but who would not cease to be, nevertheless, in some sense, a monster.
7 Roughly speaking, the black decade spans the period from the death of Juan Domingo Peron on July 1, 1974 and the military coup d´etat on March 24th, 1976 to the beginning of Alfonsin's elected democratic government on December 10th, 1983.

References

Abraham, A., & Torok, M. (2005). *La corteza y el núcleo*. Amorrortu.
Berezin, A., & García Reinoso, G. (2010). Resiliencia o la selección del más apto. ¿Ideología y práctica del aguante. In A. Berezin (Ed.), *Sobre la crueldad. La oscuridad en los ojos*. Paidós. 52–81.
Bowlby, J. (1973). *Attachment and loss* (3 vols.). Basic Books.

Caruth, C. (Ed.). (1995). *Trauma: Explorations in memory*. Johns Hopkins University Press.
Caruth, C. (1996). *Unclaimed experience: Trauma, narrative and history*. Johns Hopkins University Press.
CINTRAS, EATIP, GTNM/RJ & SERSOC. (2009). *Daño transgeneracional: Consecuencias de la represión política en el Cono Sur*. Gráfica LOM.
Danieli, Y. (Ed.). (1998). *International handbook of multigenerational legacies of trauma*. Plenum Press.
Edelman, G. M., & Tononi, G. (2000). *A universe of consciousness: How matter becomes imagination*. Basic Books.
Feierstein, D. (2014). *Genocide as social practice: Reorganizing society under Nazism and Argentina´s military juntas*. Rutgers University Press. (Spanish original version: *El genocidio como práctica social: entre el nazismo y la experiencia argentina*, Buenos Aires, FCE, 2007).
Fonagy, P. (2003). Psychoanalysis today. *World Psychiatry: Official Journal of the World Psychiatric Association (WPA)*, 2(2), 73–80.
Freud, S. (1936). *Inhibitions, symptoms and anxiety*. The Hogarth Press and the Institute of Psycho-analysis.
Freud, S. (2008). *General psychological theory: Papers on metapsychology*. Touchstone/Simon & Schuster.
Gudehus, C., Eichenberg, A., & Welzer, H. (Eds.) (2010). *Gedächtnis und Erinnerung. Ein interdisziplinares Handbuch*. Metzler.
Hartmann, E. (1996). Who develops PTSD nightmares and who doesn't. In D. Barrett (Ed.), *Trauma and dreams* (pp. 100–113). Cambridge University Press.
Käes, R. (1976). *L´Appareil psychique groupal. Constructions du groupe*. Bordas Dunod.
Käes, R. (2007). *Un singulier pluriel. La psychanalisé á l´épreuve du groupe*. Dunod.
Kaës, R., Faimberg, H., Enriquez, M., & Baranes, J. J. (1996). *Transmisión de la vida psíquica entre generaciones*. Amorrortu.
Kirsch, M., & Mertens, W. (2018). On the drive specificity of Freudian drives for the generation of seeking activities: The importance of the underestimated imperative motor factor. *Frontiers in Psychology*, 9, 616. https://doi.org/10.3389/fpsyg.2018.00616
Kordon, D., Edelman, E., Lagos, D., & Kersner, D. (2012). *South, dictatorship and after: Psychosocial and clinical elaboration of collective traumas*. EATIP Argentine Team of Psychosocial Work and Research. http://www.eatip.org.ar/wp-content/uploads/2012/06/South-dictatorship-and-after...-Psychosocial-and-clinical-elaboration-of-collective-traumas.pdf
Lacan, J. (1994). *The four fundamental concepts of psychoanalysis* (Alan Sheridan, Trans.). Penguin.
LaCapra, D. (1998). *History and memory after Auschwitz*. Cornell University Press.
Lansky, M., & Bley, C. (1995). *Posttraumatic nightmares: Psychodynamic explorations*. Hillsdale.
Laplanche, J., & Pontalis, J. B. (1988). *The language of psycho-analysis* (Donald Nicholson-Smith, Trans.). Karnac.
Leys, R. (2000). *Trauma: A genealogy*. University of Chicago Press.
Masling, J. (1960). The influence of situational and interpersonal variables in projective testing. *Psychological Bulletin*, 57, 65–85.

Piaget, P. (1985). *The equilibration of cognitive structures: The Central problem of intellectual development*. University of Chicago Press.

Puget, J., & Kaës, R. (Eds.) (1991). *Violencia de Estado y psicoanálisis*. Lumen.

Robben, A. (2008). *Pegar donde más duele. Violencia política y trauma social en Argentina*. Anthropos.

Strachey, & A. Freud (Eds.), *The standard edition of the complete psychological works of Sigmund Freud*. The Hogarth Press and the Institute of Psycho-Analisis, 24 volumes.

Van Der Kolk, B. (1998). Trauma and memory. *Psychiatry and Clinical Neurosciences, 52*, S52–S64. https://doi.org/10.1046/j.1440-1819.1998.0520s5S97.x

Van der Kolk, B., Blitz, R., Burr, W., Sherry, S., & Hartmann, E. (1984). Nightmares and trauma: A comparison of nightmares after combat with life-long nightmares in veterans. *American Journal of Psychiatry, 141*, 187–190.

3
MEMORY PROCESSES IN THE SOCIAL SCIENCES, HISTORY AND PHILOSOPHY

Philosophical reflections on memory cover a vast time span from antiquity to the present day. The topic has attracted thinkers from Plato and Aristotle, through Saint Augustine, to Bergson, Halbwachs and Ricoeur (Cassel et al., 2013). Consequently, any discussion of the philosophy of memory must necessarily be partial and subjective. Here I will focus on discussions that contribute to the objective of this first volume: a social and political account of the memory processes involved in working through the catastrophic trauma of genocide or mass killing.

As in previous chapters, then, no attempt will be made to cover the literature on memory exhaustively, but only that which is essential to the task in hand. The chapter will start with Henri Bergson's hypotheses on the relationship between memory and action. It will also draw on concepts from sociologists and social psychologists such as Maurice Halbwachs, Frederic Bartlett and Jan Assmann before returning to philosophy and the work of Paul Ricœur, in particular his concept of "narrative identity."

This chapter will also consider the work of an author at the crossroads of philosophical and sociological inquiry: Walter Benjamin. Like Kandel and Edelman in neuroscience or Freud in psychoanalysis, Walter Benjamin shines like a beacon in the field of the philosophy of history, particularly when it comes to differentiating history from memory or questioning the status of testimony as a source for historical reconstruction.

Henri Bergson, the relationship between memory and action: A reflection on absence and consciousness

Henri Bergson's *Matter and Memory* first appeared in 1895, the same year that Freud published his *Project for a Scientific Psychology for Neurologists and Psychologists* along with some of his foundational works of psychoanalysis. We have already explored several of Freud's concepts in the previous chapter and we will come back to these later in this chapter. Ten years after *Matter and Memory*, Bergson went on to publish *Creative Evolution*, in which he reflects more deeply on the peculiar connection between past and present – a present where memory serves as a tool for action – and the way in which human consciousness can be understood based on this relationship.

A fundamental principle of Bergson's philosophy is that perception and memory are intrinsically linked to present action. A sentence from *Matter and Memory* sums this up succinctly: "You define the present in an arbitrary manner as *that which is*, whereas the present is simply *what is being made*" (Bergson, 1919). The past subsists in us as a tool for present action, both through motor mechanisms and through what Bergson calls "independent memories" or "image-memories."

It will be seen that Bergson's first form of memory – specifically, that linked to motor learning and motor routines – is crucial to understanding many recent developments in neuroscience, some of which are discussed in Chapter 1. The second, by contrast, requires a more complex understanding, as reality turns out to be even stranger than even Bergson himself could have imagined. Indeed, current neuroscientific thinking does not even come close to Bergson's concept of "image-memories." Instead, we have snippets or fragments of perceived experiences spread across multiple memory systems (sensory, semantic, episodic, etc.) that become "scenes" only when they are reconstructed in a clearly creative process. This process is more similar to our everyday concept of imagination than to the classical view of memory as a *store* consolidated over time. This process, moreover, is intersubjective – that is, it is shared between two or more people.

Indeed, Bergson had already tried in *Matter and Memory* to work out the link between "image-memories" and imagination. However, given the historical period in which he was writing, he was unable to break with the notion of human memory as a store that becomes progressively *fixed* over time, a notion supported by a series of experiments conducted by Georg Elias Müller and Alfons Pilzecker at the University of Göttingen between 1892 and 1900 (Prado-Alcala & Quirarte, 2007).

In a modern version of the theory of memory consolidation, Winocur and Moscovitch (2011) claim that a new memory trace is added and serves to reinforce and strengthen memory each time a memory is retrieved in the hippocampus. However, as expressed by Edelman (in Chapter 1), each time a memory is retrieved, we are really returning to the last time we remembered the scene or the event and not to the original experience, which may have been substantially different.

Another of Bergson's enriching concepts is his understanding of consciousness as "an arithmetical difference between potential and real activity. [...]

the interval between representation and action" (Bergson, 1944 [1911], p. 160). Unlike instinct, which is unconscious, Bergson considers intelligence to be a distinctively human attribute. Intelligence is qualitatively different from instinct since it implies the ability to make conscious choices by imagining different paths of action. Memory contributes to this process by providing various options from the past. In this way, the will is also freed from historical or unconscious conditioning and can play a role in integrating the past into present action.

For Bergson, one of the tools that can free human beings from automatic behavior – behavior performed without conscious self-control – is language. Language "furnishes consciousness with an immaterial body in which to incarnate itself and thus exempts it from dwelling exclusively on material bodies, whose flux would soon drag it along and finally swallow it up" (Bergson, 1944 [1911], p. 288). There is a striking parallel between the way Bergson understands the relationship between language and consciousness and Freud's idea of *word-representation* and working through (*Durcharbeiten*) as a way of escaping from repetition compulsion, or from automatically reenacting the past.

The profundity of Bergson's philosophy, however, becomes more clear when he analyzes the implications of *absence* for the processes of consciousness and memory:

> A being unendowed with memory or prevision would not use the words "void" or "nought"; he *[sic]* would express only what is and what is perceived; now, what is, and what is perceived, is the presence of one thing or of another, never the absence of anything. There is absence only for a being capable of remembering and expecting. [...]. It is only a comparison between what is and what could or ought to be, between the full and the full.
>
> *(Bergson, 1944 [1911], pp. 306–307)*

For Bergson, it is precisely memory that makes absence possible: the absence of *what once was*, of *the no longer present* (in the form of mourning, melancholy or legacy), but also the absence of the *not yet present* (in the form of hope or expectation).

It is reasonable to suppose, then, that if memory constructs the presence of what is absent, *what has been destroyed* should persist as a gap in the present. Thanks to memory, destruction does not necessarily imply an immediate disappearance from the realm of consciousness.

Although Bergson never addressed the problem of mass destruction, it is clear that what has been destroyed by genocide, and even the possibility of remembering what has been destroyed, does not disappear without further ado. To erase a thing, a state, a feeling or a social bond, it is not enough simply to destroy it, for it will continue to exist in the present as an empty place in memory. For something to disappear definitively, its absence – which is also a sort of empty presence – must be replaced by something else, another presence, much as for example Halloween, Christmas and New Year's Eve replaced earlier pagan festivals.

Elsewhere, I refer to the "symbolic enactment" of genocidal social practices which follows the physical annihilation of the victim and drives survivor groups or societies to fill the void of absence with new meanings (Feierstein, 2000, 2014). I also discuss the ways in which these meanings are linked to the need for action by being woven into new webs of social relations. In other words, when a group, a social identity, and a specific "way of being-in-the-world," is destroyed, the absence remains present; an absence that calls on historians or social scientists to read and interpret what is present in terms of what is absent, what could not be.

The symbolic enactment of a genocide attempts to fill the void of absence with a network of new representations, symbolically erasing what had already been materially destroyed. The new presence gradually obliterates all trace of the old, and the presence of what is absent gradually fades away, blocking the process of mourning and working-through the trauma.

The social frameworks of memory

Writing only a decade or two after Bergson, Maurice Halbwachs studied with both Bergson himself and with the sociologist Émile Durkheim. Consequently, a basic tenet of Halbwachs' work is that social events are qualitatively different from the sum of individual events. This classic Durkheimian approach is clearly seen in his critique of the concept of "image-memories," one of the weakest points in Bergson's theory of memory processes.

Today, Halbwachs is considered a classic in the history of sociology, especially for his work on collective memory and the "social frameworks of memory," published in 1925. Sadly, Bergson does not enjoy the same prestige as Halbwachs. Historical or sociological works on memory often start with Halbwachs, as if unaware of the depth and significance of his predecessor's work.

The previous chapters in this book suggest that what was a novelty in Halbwachs' work at the beginning of the twentieth century – the possibility of a "collective memory" – has become almost a cliché in the 21st century. This is largely because a variety of disciplines has begun to challenge the notion of individual memory – the flipside of collective memory. It is therefore particularly significant that neuroscience, psychoanalysis and the social sciences agree in considering memory as both a creative reconstruction and a social process. In this sense, the distinction between individual and collective memory becomes meaningless, since all memory is ultimately social and historical in nature and, therefore, collective. Halbwachs expresses this unity between the individual and the social in the conclusion of his book *The Social Frameworks of Memory* just as Bergson had done, even if the latter did not take such a radical stance. In Halbwachs' own words:

> There are hence no perceptions without recollections. But, inversely, there are no recollections which can be said to be purely interior, that is, which can be preserved only within individual memory. Indeed, from the moment that a recollection reproduces a collective perception, it can itself only be collective; it would be impossible for the individual to represent to himself anew, using only his forces, that which he could not represent to himself previously – unless he has recourse to the thought of his group. [...] There is hence no memory without perception. As soon as we locate people in society it is no longer possible to distinguish two types of observations, one exterior, the other interior.
> *(Halbwachs, 1992, pp. 168–169)*

The idea of "social frameworks" (*cadres sociaux*) of memory is incisive and profound, and is one of the author's major contributions. Halbwachs understands these elements – place, form, name and reflection – as instruments that make it possible to fix memories, and give them meaning and distinctiveness by linking them to other elements that appear to be more fixed or stable. This notion allows us to analyze the types of meaning that make up the memory of genocidal experiences. Nevertheless, social frameworks – the structures on which subsequent processes of memory are based – are also constructed collectively. They simply have a greater degree of historical sedimentation, which is what gives them a certain fixity and solidity.

Social frameworks are thus points of reference. Constructed in social institutions such as the family, religious groups or social classes, among others, they make it possible to capture and make sense of personal life experiences. These are then inscribed as memory. Through a work of creative reconstruction guided by the imagination, they come to occupy a place both defined and constrained by these frames of reference. They become linked to ways of understanding and constructing meaning that are rooted in the group's experience of the historical past sedimented as *a common history*, as a *collective history*.

Consequently, Halbwachs does not equate remembering with *reliving* the past. Rather, the practice of remembering *reconstructs* the past out of the social frameworks of the present. This notion – like those found in neuroscience or psychoanalysis – is closely linked to Piaget's theory of equilibration, which involves altering one's existing ideas about the world in response to new information and experiences.

Writing in the same vein, Jan and Aleida Assmann have introduced two new terms to think about these processes: "communicative memory" and "cultural memory." Communicative memory represents an interpersonal way of understanding social memory, shaped by emotions, feelings of belonging, shame, etc., which give precision and horizon to our memories. Communicative memory is directed toward another individual. Assmann says in this respect that "[...] longing for attention and the wish to belong is active in every memory. The socialization process enables us to remember, but the converse is also true: our memories help us to become socialized. [...] We can go so far as to speak of a 'bonding memory'" (Assmann, 2006, p. 4).

At the same time, Assmann sets out to demolish the customary distinction between memory and tradition by coining the term "cultural memory" for a specific type of "communicative memory." Cultural memory is created when the past is transmitted from one generation to another. This specific type of bonding memory linked to generational transmission creates a system of traces that makes communal identity possible.

Social frameworks of memory and their sedimented forms – whether traditional, cultural or communicative – make our understanding of the *social* and *political* nature of memory both richer and more precise. This is in addition to the *constructive* and *imaginative* nature of memory we have already considered.

Bartlett: Experiments in memory transmission

Sir Frederic Bartlett was the first professor of experimental psychology at the University of Cambridge and a contemporary of Halbwachs. In his classic work *Remembering* (1932), Bartlett presented numerous experiments suggesting that memories of past events and experiences are actually mental reconstructions. These experiments studied participants' ability to reproduce short stories, informational texts, images or perceptions over a period of days, weeks, months or years and/or what happened when messages were transmitted from one person to another.

Bartlett's conclusions have much in common with the neuroscientific hypotheses developed by Edelman, Kandel or Changeux 50 to 80 years later and explained in Chapter 1 of this book. Bartlett's most important conclusion was, of course, that memory reconstructs events rather than simply reproducing them. In other words, it involves a process of creation or imagination. However, and in line with Halbwachs, Bartlett also emphasizes the essentially *social* nature of this process. In other words, memory is constructed *with others* and *thanks to others*.

Bartlett explored three different processes – perception, imagination and memory – using three different research methods: description, repeated reproduction and serial reproduction. With description and repeated reproduction, participants repeatedly retrieved the same memory over time. With serial reproduction, one person read a set of information before reproducing it for another person, who then reproduced it for a third person and so on.

Bartlett found that existing information was reconstructed in terms of meaning. Far from being reproduced literally, elements were added, removed or distorted in order to create coherence within a memory (e.g., of a text or a series of faces) and between the memory and the person's experience (the sedimented social frameworks from which it is interpreted, a classic Halbwachs construction).

In his experiments on perception, Bartlett worked on vision, but his approach could equally be applied to other types of perception such as hearing. Bartlett discovered that what was perceived depended on pre-existing mental images (schema), language (verbalization), affective/attitude aspects, and social and cultural contexts. He emphasized the "inferential processes" involved in perception – in other words, that what is perceived is not actually present, but is added by the observer to make sense of what is observed. This is analogous to Bergson's perception of absence, or Piaget's theory of equilibration, in which we adjust our cognitive structures to incorporate new elements from the environment (accommodation) but also transform the environment to fit pre-existing cognitive structures (assimilation).

The large part of Bartlett's work, however, deals with memory rather than perception. To this end, he conducted experiments on the recall of sequences of drawings, photographs and images, as well as short stories, informative texts and sports reports, among others. What is noticeable in all these experiments is that exact or literal recall was almost nonexistent. On the contrary, Bartlett discovered that people tended to conventionalize the features of faces or stories. This occurred with narratives whether they were mythical stories, short informative texts or sports chronicles. The number of errors was largely unaffected by the content of the story or the situation to be remembered.

Nevertheless, although Bartlett's studies suggest that literal recall does not exist, this does not mean that errors and distortions are equally distributed among all people or in all situations. There were subjects who tended to synthesize what they perceived, but maintained the gist. Others remembered names accurately but transformed the ultimate meaning of the story to a surprising extent. Yet others preserved the meaning of the story, but added numerous elements that clarified and reinforced its underlying logic.

Bartlett provided overwhelming proof that memories are distorted by being recalled repeatedly over time or by being transmitted almost simultaneously from one person to another (as in the game of Chinese whispers). This empirical evidence should have discredited the idea of reproductive memory once and for all. Only a fetishistic veneration for the "hard sciences" of chemistry and biology can explain why scientists have found neuroscientific evidence more conclusive than Bartlett's experiments.

In synthesis, several elements of Bartlett's experiments are worth highlighting:

1 Firstly, subjects forgot, distorted, reconstructed and added details without being aware of it. That is to say, they did their best to reproduce drawings and texts as accurately as possible, but it was not enough. The unconscious nature of these mistakes is fully compatible with Freud's work as we shall see later.
2 The details that subjects forgot, distorted, reconstructed or added were by no means random or the same for all subjects. Rather, they were determined by the native language and culture of each subject and by the way in which the subject's personal and social conflicts resonated with elements in the text to be recalled. Some of the differences found have already analyzed within a psychoanalytic framework, which suggests that this approach could be extended to the rest. Certainly, a psychoanalytic approach seems more promising than a probabilistic one, because the differences do not follow probabilistic patterns. In other words, inaccuracies are not evenly distributed across subjects.
3 However, it is possible to find some common patterns deriving from the subjects' tendency to search for meaning, both in drawings and narrated stories. These include: (a) a tendency to transform the incomprehensible into more conventionally accepted representations; (b) a tendency to connect "incoherent" material to create "meaningful" material, even though this may permanently erase other details of the drawings and narrated stories; (c) simplification: the permanent reduction of the complex to the simple and (d) the preservation of specific details (even if these end up acquiring new meanings).
4 Bartlett's experiments are largely compatible with Piaget's hypotheses about "equilibration systems" that describe how new information is balanced with existing knowledge. Equilibration involves the processes of assimilation (fitting new information into existing mental schemas) and accommodation (adjusting or changing a schema to fit new information). In this way, memory processes are one more element of this interplay between schemas and perceptions. We tend to notice things that fit into our schemas and ignore those that do not until the latter can be ignored no longer.

Another important conclusion of Bartlett's work was that literal recall would be much less useful in evolutionary terms than the creative memory he had found in his experiments. As he himself put it, "In a world of constantly changing environment, literal recall is extraordinarily unimportant" (Bartlett, 1932, p. 204). Thus, our inability to lay down fixed, unchanging memories is not a failure of evolution but, on the contrary, an evolutionary adaptation based on the plasticity of the neural system. In this, Bartlett pioneered a notion that would not become commonplace until the 21 century – what Edelman characterizes as the *degenerative* functioning of brain structure and Changeux as the "selective stabilization of synapses."

Bartlett illustrates his thesis by referring to the specific strokes that must be remembered at the motor level in sports such as tennis, golf or baseball. In all of these games, an infinite number of factors must be taken into account. The same shot will not necessarily produce the same effect in every match. Everything depends on where the player is standing, the state of the court or course, the wind, etc.

In other areas of life, too, each situation is to some extent unique. Now, it is extremely interesting that this "degenerative" creative system handles new situations much more effectively than computer simulations that select previously successful moves according to a set of variables. To deal with life successfully, we do not need rigid and unchangeable representations of past situations. Nor are our brains capable of computing all the possible variables we may encounter. On the contrary, in order to deal with new situations – which are similar but never entirely identical to those of the past – we need to interpret them creatively.

Bartlett considers remembering to be intertwined with imagination, and argues that the difference between the two is one of degree rather than quality. According to Bartlett, "Remembering is not the re-excitation of innumerable fixed, lifeless and fragmentary traces. It is an imaginative reconstruction or construction, built out of the relation of our attitude towards a whole active mass of organised past reactions or experience [i.e., schemata], and to a little outstanding detail which commonly appears in image or in language form" (Bartlett, 1932, p. 213).

In conclusion, Bartlett's approach dealt a severe blow to positivist theories of truth, particularly those which saw memory as a store of perceptions. Modern neuroscience suggests that Bartlett provides a vital link between neuroscience, psychoanalysis, social sciences and social psychology, given that memory is linked to creativity and imagination and that subjectivity is present even in the primary process of perception. Bartlett's findings fit perfectly with those of his contemporary Halbwachs, since this subjectivity is constructed socially as well as individually.

Revisiting the old debate between history and memory

These reflections on the nature of memory may shed light for historians on one of the most widely debated topics of the past half century, namely how we relate to the past. The debate has spread recently to other disciplines, as scholars attemp to distinguish "memory" from "history" and explore the ways historians and social scientists relate to their discipline and their material.

Even though most scholars treat memory and history as qualitatively different, there have also been attempts to find common ground between the two fields.[1] Despite their methodological differences, both fields share a concern with the nature of truth, fidelity and literality. Paul Ricœur, for example, claims that the goal of history is truth, while the goal of memory is "fidelity" (Ricœur, 2004). However, as we have seen, neuroscience, psychoanalysis and the social sciences all support the notion that that human memory is not a literal reproduction of the past but an imaginative and creative reconstruction of the past in the present. In other words, memory always involves constructing a "remembered present." This dynamic use of the past fits poorly with closed concepts such as truth and fidelity.

One important question, then, is whether this creative use of the past is limited to what historians call "memory," or whether "history" is also saturated with subjectivity and creativity. If only memory is subjective and creative, Ricœur's goal of "fidelity" is unattainable; if history is also subjective and creative, then Ricœur's goal of "truth" is equally unattainable. However, few historians would wish to give up on the ideal of truth altogether. To avoid radical skepticism, we need to establish ways of knowing whether we are getting closer to the truth, such as historical discourse analysis, subjectivity analysis and transference analysis.

This section aims, in part, to question whether it is even possible to construct a "transparent" account of the past in which the facts speak for themselves. The conservative view, based on authors such as Leopold von Ranke, holds that it *is* possible to dispense with the fictional and imaginative parts of memory. "Objective historiography," or empirically based narrative history, is thus a last bastion of positivism against the notion of history as fiction, a notion whose most provocative and irritating exponent has been Hayden White.

Here, the debate will be revisited with particular reference to what historians describe as "traumatic pasts." Far from seeking to protect history from the imaginative and creative processes of memory, I shall attempt to determine to what degree such processes are essential to the discipline of history. If there is indeed a difference between history and memory, it is unlikely to be based on Ricœur's fidelity-truth distinction.

Walter Benjamin, in his *Theses on the Philosophy of History* (Benjamin, 1969), addressed this problem long before it became a commonplace in academia. Benjamin did not accept the notion of history as correcting, interpreting or objectively analyzing memory. Although all his theses revolve around this same question, I will take just two of them that deal with the role of absence, a topic already raised by Bergson.

In Thesis VI, Benjamin argues that "to articulate the past historically does not mean 'to know it as it really was' (Ranke). It means to seize hold of a memory as it flashes up at a moment of danger" (Benjamin, 1969, p. 255).

This thesis, with its explicit critique of Ranke, is linked to Thesis XVII. The latter, as Benjamin says in a letter to Gretel Adorno, lies at the heart of his work:

> A historical materialist approaches a historical subject only where he encounters it as a monad. In this structure he recognises the sign of a Messianic cessation of happening or, put differently, a revolutionary chance in the fight for the oppressed past. He tales cognizance of it in order to blast a specific era out of the homogeneous course of history – blasting a specific life out of the era or a specific work out of the lifework. As a result of this method the lifework is preserved in this work and at the same time cancelled[2]; in the lifework, the era; and in the era, the entire course of history. The nourishing fruit of the historically understood contains time as a precious but tasteless seed.
> *(Benjamin, 1969, p. 263)*

Manuel Reyes Mate clarifies and expands the meaning of this fundamental thesis and Benjamin's rejection of "objective historiography" or empirically based narrative history. As Reyes Mate says: "Objective historiography gets it wrong because it lacks theoretical nerve: it constructs universality by adding up data. In this way it will not get very far because in history data are only a part of reality. It must also tell what did not come to be." And, further on, he adds:

> For Benjamin the explanation of what was lost is not enough to go ahead with the interpretation of universal history [...] There is no longer any universality possible if what is left out is hermeneutically unimportant [...] The amputated does not heal with an interpretation in which the concrete, traumatic event is subsumed in the logic of the whole [...] The marginal becomes a privileged observatory of the process as a whole.
> *(Reyes Mate, 2006, pp. 262–266)*

Reyes Mate recalls how Benjamin cites Péguy in his critique of objective historiography, more precisely Péguy's attempt to analyze Henri Bergson. Referring to historians in general, Péguy argued that "they have made themselves the archivists of the world, but it has been in order to squander the archives. They have become the treasurers of the world, but to squander its treasures. They have become the accountants of mankind, but to constantly increase the debits and credits" (Reyes Mate, 2006, p. 271).

It is Benjamin himself who rounds off the critique of historical objectivity, with its search for a universal and global truth, in fragment A of thesis XIX:

> Historical objectivity contents itself with establishing a causal link between various moments in history. But no fact that is a cause is for that very

reason historical. It becomes historical posthumously, as it were, through events which may be separated from it by thousands of years. A historian who takes this as his *[sic]* point of departure stops telling the sequence of events like the beads of a rosary. Instead, he grasps the constellation which his epoch has formed with a definite earlier one. Thus, he establishes a conception of the present as "the time of the now" which is shot through with chips of messianic time.

(Benjamin, 1969, p. 263)

Recorded during the dark days of early 1940, Benjamin's insights are supported by disciplines quite different from his own, although compatible with his political aims and concerns. Indeed, everything I have presented from the most diverse disciplines has sought to respect a fundamental principle of Benjamin's work: to construct a "history of the vanquished" as a history of what did not come to be.

Questioning the notion of history as a field *beyond* memory

One of the best summaries of the debate on how to represent mass state violence (whether as memory and/or history) can be found in Saul Friedländer's classic compilation *Probing the Limits of Representation. Nazism and the "Final Solution"* (Friedländer, 1992). Indeed, this book has still not been bettered after 30 years. A large part of the debate hinges on Hayden White's criticism of historicism, and the book presents not only Friedländer's own position but those of Carlo Ginzburg, Perry Anderson, Amos Funkenstein, Christopher Browning, Dan Diner, Dominick LaCapra and Berel Lang, among others – all experts in the fields of history and the social sciences.

Beyond a now relatively outdated discussion on the greater or lesser validity of oral sources for history, the key issue is whether an event can be reassembled like a jigsaw puzzle – that is, "as it happened" and "letting the facts speak for themselves." If this is not possible, we need to disentangle the subjective process of memory, the search for objectivity that guides the historian's work and the historian's reliance on literary discourse for creating meaning. Hayden White's analysis of this last issue has been particularly enlightening.

Depending on one's position, the differences between history and memory could lie in the way questions are framed since historical questions or problems help historians select, analyze and organize information. But they could also lie in the type of primary sources, the sources used to check them against or the type of narrative chosen. To help clarify this problem, I will now consider in turn the sources, aims, methods and habitual forms of representation in history and memory studies.

The question of sources

Given that historical events are no longer directly observable but must be mediated by evidence of some kind, it is difficult to understand why historians' use of primary sources should differ qualitatively from the procedures used to construct a collective memory. Historians have no access to the events themselves, only to representations of the events. This is true whether they work with "documents" – reified traces in text, image or sound of representations closer to the original events – or "oral histories" – stories that they have been told repeatedly with all the distortions identified by Bartlett.

Subjectivity is always present whenever an artist creates a novel or a painting. The same is just as true when a historical participant, journalist or photographer creates a document, article or image. Consequently, such documents, even when reified as belonging to a precise historical moment, are already a "representation" of reality relying on one or more levels of mediation and not reality itself. This is the raw material of every historian, a record as mediated as any other memory. True: the number of mediations may be fewer; but this cannot be taken for granted and needs to be confirmed in each individual case.

Michael Pollak sums this point up clearly:

> The historian's work is always done on the basis of some source. It is obvious that the construction we make of the past, even the most positivist construction, is always dependent on the intermediation of the document. To the extent that this intermediation is unavoidable, all the historian's work is based on an initial reconstruction. I think that we can no longer remain, from an epistemological point of view, tied to a primary positivist naivety. I don't think there are many people today who defend that position.
>
> *(Pollak, 1989, pp. 3–15)*

An exception to this claim might be performative documents, such as a law, a decree, or an order for kidnapping, deportation, assassination and so forth. Because of their official nature, these documents constitute a form of social action.

But there are also some caveats to be noted with regard to the latter. On the one hand, such documents are generally not sufficient for the historian, since leaders and high-ranking officials rarely leave evidence of their plans for mass murder in black and white. Such orders have usually been given orally, especially since the Nuremberg trials. Lower-ranking officials may give orders in writing, but this is usually done using euphemisms that require interpretation by the historian, who must replace these euphemisms with the actions they symbolize.[3]

As has already been pointed out, these documents are uncommon. They are usually treated by the historian as just one more to be added to the set of representations of the facts, which in some cases are reified to the point of being treated as if they were the concrete real event.

And here I would like to pause for a moment to make something completely clear. Questioning our ability to reproduce an event exactly as it happened should not lead us into the relativist trap of believing that reality is mere interpretation. That is not the point I wish to make, and I eschew any sort of radical epistemological relativism or philosophical idealism.

Reality does exist. Its material nature is unquestionable. And it exists beyond any of its interpretations, whatever the level of mediation. I say this because there is a real risk in questioning the status of historical inquiry we may end up in a sort of narrative idealism, claiming that reality does not exist.

What I want to make clear is that our experience of past reality is always mediated by processes of representation. Not only that, all access to the past is determined by the needs and uses of that past in the present. Thus, the historian's approach to reality is necessarily subjective, both as a result of conscious decisions and, more importantly, unconscious processes. It is important, then, to critically analyze our ability to take on board our complex relationship with the past, *both* in the field of memory *and* in the field of history.

Carlo Guinzburg, one of the greatest contemporary defenders of the "evidential paradigm," has been a staunch critic of Hayden White. Nevertheless, Guinzburg recognizes that historical knowledge is *indirect, conjectural* and *interpretative*. The documents with which the historian work are not pieces of reality but rather representations of the past which historians evaluate and compare, and from which they infer certain events. This painstaking work of reconstruction (whether Guinzburg acknowledges it or not) is a creative process (Friedländer, 1992).

Now, as we have seen, this is precisely the way memory works. Memory, too, draws on fragmentary representations of the past (belonging to the individual or to others) to produce an adaptation of the past to the present that is *indirect, conjectural* and *interpretative*. There does not seem to be much difference, then, between memory and history at this first level of sources.

Performative sources are rare and not directly a part of reality, although they can provide material for both history and memory. On the other hand, other sources – those which generally form the basis of history and memory – involve representations of reality that are mediated to a greater or lesser degree. Yet, being mere sources, they cannot be fundamental for distinguishing memory processes from the work of historians.

This does not mean giving up on the ethical desire for truth, which is at the heart of history's claim to be a discipline and even at the heart of its link to justice as its guiding horizon. However, the desire for truth does not, of itself, serve to differentiate history from memory, given that the same desire is present in both endeavors.

We will now examine the explicit and implicit aims of history and memory studies in order to see whether these can provide more conclusive evidence of a difference between the two.

The question of objectives

The second question is whether the purpose of memory (the creation of a "remembered present" linked to a need for action) might be qualitatively different from the purposes of the historian or social scientist. Here, it is important to stress that, just as the manifest function of memory (remembering the past) does not coincide with its latent function (action in the present), an analogous situation may be found in the so-called search for historical truth. To what extent is it really a search for patterns in the *present* and thus an attempt to understand and solve current and future problems?

Certainly, historians need to examine the conditioning factors of their time and – if history is not to be viewed as something closed and complete – they need to be aware of what they project unconsciously onto their area of study. Dominick LaCapra suggests that historians should approach the past, especially traumatic events such as war and genocide, in the same way that patients approach a psychoanalytic cure. In other words, they should work through them in the present in order to complete the work of mourning effectively and produce positive results in the future (LaCapra, 1998).

When we remember, we think we are diving into the past and retrieving a previously classified memory. This task often seems to have no meaning beyond itself. However, Edelman, Freud, Piaget and Bartlett all suggest that what we really do is transform traces from various memory systems into something that changes slightly each time we remember it, like the Chinese whispers in Bartlett's experiments. Or to revisit Edelman's metaphor: a glacier that melts and refreezes each time an act of remembering is attempted (Edelman & Tononi, 2000).

The raw data are probably there: a face, a smell, a pain, a suffering and a sensation; but in assembling these data into a scene, into a story, we are already engaging in a creative act. This is true whether we are aware of it or believe we are retrieving something unchanged from memory. Remembering is always a way of updating the past, consciously or unconsciously, in order to act on it. Or as Bergson would have it, the past is reconstructed in order to serve as a *tool* for the present.

The historian's task is similar. The explicit aim is to document and narrate a historical period, but the time period to be covered, the relative importance given to different sources and the types of narration chosen, among other things, are all personal decisions. Based on clinical and other evidence,

LaCapra argues that these elements satisfy the historian's present needs through what he calls "relations of transference" with the subject matter. Again, this is irrespective of whether the historian's conscious aim is to "get to the truth."

Of course, naive historians and social scientists may deny any transference on their part and insist that their sole aim is truth. Nowadays, however, most historians and social scientists are trained to reflect critically on their assumptions, as well as the way they are positioned by personal, family and social-historical factors. This sort of critical epistemological awareness can indeed make a difference. Scholars who become *aware* of their motivations and limitations are able to become ethically responsible for the consequences of their work. But in any case, this does not make the objectives of history different from those of memory, but it is rather linked to the way historians work.

In conclusion, there is no substantial difference between history and memory at the level of objectives, either. Whether an eyewitness is recalling a specific experience, or a historian is constructing a broader view of the past, both are using the past to act in the present. They may do so in interpersonal ways (as in the case of eyewitness memory) or in broader social ways (as in the case of history or social science) but their purposes are substantially the same.

Let us turn now to the level of procedures, which may provide a firmer basis for a distinction between memory and history.

The question of methodology or procedures

What makes history a discipline is precisely its specific way of dealing with primary sources. Consequently, we would expect to find more important differences between memory and history at this third level – methodology and procedures.

Historians are forced to check their hypotheses against other sources and interpretations, and must constantly revise the representations they construct. This imposes limits on the ways that documents and the other raw material of history can be interpreted. This sort of control is not impossible when dealing with memory, but it could be argued that witnesses construct their representations in a much more spontaneous manner, and that there is no systematic way to resolve discrepancies either between different memories or between different interpretations of the same memories.

History, on the other hand, provides frameworks for clearly defined discussions as well as identifying legitimate and illegitimate ways of interpreting and analyzing sources, legitimate and illegitimate ways of constructing a particular record as a source and legitimate and illegitimate ways of inferring hypotheses from sources.

Does this difference in methodology amount to a difference in objectives or horizons? I have already suggested that it does not. The procedures of memory and history may be different but both are subject to similar distortions and limitations. These include the author's transference to the subject matter, repressed material operating unconsciously, the creative nature of interpretation and the distortions of reality present in the sources themselves, among others. However, all this does not detract from the rich traditions of critical and historical inquiry, including its development of a metadiscourse – that is, an ongoing discussion on *how* to approach history. Such discussions are much less common in memory studies.

The disciplinary nature of history means that history not only *can* but *should* be critical. This is much more difficult in an interpersonal and spontaneous process such as memory or in a field such as memory studies, which spans many disciplines and uses very diverse methods (Bosch, 2016).

To those who aspire to objectivity and truth, reducing the difference between history and memory to a set of procedures for validating one's conclusions may seem to trivialize history. But these procedures are by no means trivial when one considers how histories of the Holocaust – the paradigmatic case of genocide – have contributed to constructing individual and collective memory. Not only have they contributed new facts and new sources but also new interpretations, and they have built up a body of documents and testimonies that no memory process – however affected it may be by the existence of negative pacts – can end up ignoring. This collective body of documentation on the Nazi genocides has created a consensus in society that affects any new process of remembrance or interpretation, whatever the representation is in which this body of documents is included.

This does not, however, detract from the creative nature of the historian's or social scientist's work. On the contrary, it recognizes each person's specific contribution. If an author's work is solid and original, there will be new approach to add to the arsenal of critical tools with which to examine each new process of remembrance. All of this brings history closer to the disciplines known as "social sciences," insomuch as historians do not act very differently from sociologists, anthropologists or political scientists. These disciplines also need to be critical and self-reflective.

To sum up, the critical and self-reflective nature of history sets it apart from memory studies, with their more individual and intersubjective approaches to memory. The representations constructed by historians are generally more solid and more likely to become historically established. They constitute what Halbwachs calls "social frameworks of memory," sets of representations that support and provide a reference for individual memory processes. Nonetheless, they are still creative representations, however well-written and convincing they may be. They are exquisitely subjective uses of the past aimed at understanding the present and, as such, their purpose is eminently political.

This subjectivity in no way reduces the historian's or social scientist's ethical responsibility. On the contrary, by making the creative and tentative nature of historical interpretation explicit, writers are also forced to think about the deeper purpose and possible consequences of their work. It is not the facts that speak, but historians who make them speak. Accordingly, historians must take ethical and political responsibility for what they say. They need to be aware of why they have chosen to study a particular topic or period; why they have chosen to work with a particular set of sources; why they have made the past speak in one way and not another. This is as true for ancient as for modern history since historians can establish unconscious identifications with any historical figure or period. It is by no means certain that a history of Egyptian or Roman times can be more detached than the history of Nazi Germany or Latin American dictatorships.

Forms of representation

As mentioned earlier, one of the first and is perhaps the best-known discussions of historical narratives is that of Hayden White (White, 1973). White's success lies in having identified (and opened up for discussion) the creative nature of historical representation, the evidence (which has not gone unchallenged by many historians) that the facts do not speak for themselves but that it is the historian who makes them speak following a limited number of plot types. These plots tend to use the resources of other literary genres to construct meaning, a meaning that does not arise from the facts themselves or from the sources but is imposed by the historian.

However, White neglects the question of objectives. If memory and history cannot be separated, history and fiction certainly can. History and memory attempt to establish the truth about the past – however imperfect the result may be – and with it the possibility of healing and justice. These elements, however, are missing from fiction, where the free rein of the imagination is not necessarily accompanied by any search for truth. Fiction can allow itself to explore the unreal, the fantastic, the never-happened, even specific forms of distorted reality.

This theme has been explored in depth by Paul Ricœur, both in his three-volume classic *Time and Narrative* (Ricœur, 1984–1988) and later in *Memory, History, Forgetting* (2004). In the latter, Ricœur identifies a branch of the history of representations involving self-reflection and the construction of what might be called a *meta-history*. This branch, says Ricœur, relies on the understanding "that I am able to speak, act, recount, impute to myself the responsibility for my actions" (Ricœur, 2004, p. 132). He goes on to distinguish three levels on which historical representations operate:

1. As "remembrance," the final conclusion of the experience of reknowing, representation as memory, the construction of a scene with the recorded elements of the past;
2. As a stage of the historiographical operation that leads to the historian's representation of the past: "once the historian's labor, begun in the archives, ends in the publication of a book or an article to be read" (Ricœur, 2004, p. 132);
3. The third and the final level should be the one in which history can demonstrate whether it has resolved or simply transposed "the aporias of memory at the heart of historical knowledge" (Ricœur, 2004, p. 132). Aporia here means irreconcilable contradictions or paradoxes.

In relation to this possible third level, Ricœur says:

Between the mnemonic representation from the beginning of our discourse and the literary representation situated at the end of the trajectory of the historiographical operation, representation presents itself as an object, a referent, of the historian's discourse. Can it be that the object represented by historians bears the mark of the initial enigma of mnemonic representation and anticipates the final enigma of the historical representation of the past?
(Ricœur, 2004, p. 132)

Ricœur recognizes Hayden White's contribution to analyzing the ways history is represented. Nevertheless, he criticizes White for confusing the aims and procedures of history with those of fiction, despite the reliance of both on plotted narratives. A category mistake (or category error) is a logical fallacy where the properties of the whole are confused with the properties of a part. Ricœur considers that White commits a category mistake in extending his analogy about plot construction to the level of aims and procedures, where history and fiction are clearly differentiated.

What is suggestive is that – in terms of use of sources and implicit or explicit objectives – memory studies are much closer to history than to fiction. As I have already pointed out, it is only at the level of procedures that memory and history are different. But it is also here where their possible connections can be found: memory precedes the work of any historian, but history provides the social frameworks in which memories can be stored.

Now, it is at the level of representation that the creative character of both practices (memory and history) appears most clearly, despite the difference in their procedures. Notwithstanding Ricœur's warning about category mistakes, Hayden White's merit has been to analyze rigorously the most creative moment of historiographical work: its final result. According to White, emplotment seeks to align fragments of the past with an ideology that explains the present and guides future actions. Thus, *romance*, which celebrates the triumph of good after different setbacks, usually embodies an anarchist ideology, while *comedy*, which celebrates shared human values, usually embodies a conservative one. Similarly, *tragedy*, by showing what happens when values collide, leans toward a radical ideology, while *satire*, by stressing the role of chance and human folly in life, leans toward a liberal one.

Walter Benjamin had already argued that historian "grasps [*erfasst*] the constellation in which his own era has formed with a definite earlier one. Thus, he establishes a conception of the present as 'the time of the now' [*Jetztzeit*], which is shot through with chips of messianic time" (Benjamin, 1969, p. 263). These chips of messianic time in the present, "seize hold of a memory as it flashes in a moment of danger" (Benjamin, 1969, p. 255).

Benjamin, then, suggests a profound way of linking past and present through history. At the same time, history is linked to memory in that both activities hold the promise of justice within them. As we will see next, Ricœur takes this relationship a step further with one of his most enriching concepts: that of narrative identity.

Paul Ricœur: Linking the processes of memory and history through the concept of "narrative identity"

Time and narrative are contradictory notions because, as Ricœur points out: "stories are recounted and not lived; life is lived and not recounted" (Ricœur, 1991, p. 20). His three-volume *Time and Narrative* concludes accordingly with a threefold proposal to address the irresolvable aporias or contradictions between time and narrative. Without ignoring his poetic image of "narration as the guardian of time," we will focus on the first of these aporias: narrative identity. This is the one Ricœur himself considers to be most resilient, and whose effects and limitations he describes in the final pages of *Time and Narrative*.

Ricœur's definition of narrative identity is worth quoting briefly, not only for its clarity but also for the beauty of Ricœur's prose:

> The fragile offshoot issuing from the union of history and fiction is the assignment to an individual or a community of a specific identity that we can call their *narrative identity* (emphasis added) [...] But what is the basis for the permanence of this proper name? What justifies our taking the subject of an action, so designated by his, her, or its proper name, as the same throughout a life that stretches from birth to death? The answer has to be narrative.
>
> *(Ricœur, 1984–1988, Volume 3, p. 246)*

For Ricœur, this narrative identity is what gives continuity to one's sense of self, as well as resolving the dichotomy between "self "and "other" that runs through all of our existence. It is thus essential from an adaptive point of view and also a prerequisite for ethical existence.

Ricœur continues:

> Self-sameness, "self-constancy," can escape the dilemma of the Same and the Other to the extent that its identity rests on a temporal structure that conforms to the model of dynamic identity arising from the poetic composition of a narrative text. The self, characterized by self-sameness, may then be said to be refigured by the reflective application of such narrative configurations. Unlike the abstract identity of the Same, this narrative identity, constitutive of self-constancy, can include change, mutability, within the cohesion of one lifetime. The subject then appears both as a reader and the writer of its own life, as Proust would have it. As the literary analysis of autobiography confirms, the story of a life continues to be refigured by all the truthful or active stories a subject tells about himself or herself. This refiguration makes this life itself a cloth woven of stories told.
>
> *(Ricœur, 1984–1988, p. 246)*

The creative act of memory sets up a story at both the individual and intersubjective levels which, in time, becomes woven into a series of related stories. These stories establish causal links between what is, what has been and what could not be. We know who we are at any given moment thanks to these interwoven narratives, which shape our identities both as individuals and as peoples.

Ricœur explains that the stories we tell ourselves can be true or fictional. In the end, it is less important whether a story reflects what actually happened. For example, nearly every culture in the world has a foundation myth even if most are partly or wholly untrue. Similarly, the goal of narrative therapy is to uncover opportunities for growth and development, rather than provide an exhaustive account of the past. What is important is that stories are coherent and meaningful and maintain our sense of identity over time.

Dirk Moses analyzes how narratives intersect with suffering, trauma and conspiracy theories and how they can bring the experience of the past into the present. For example, he shows how the present-day Israeli Jewish population equates Palestinians with Nazis (Moses, 2011).

Benjamin adds an ethical imperative to this type of historical reconstruction, one that also appears in Ricœur, citing Emmanuel Levinas. In this respect, it is worth recalling Reyes Mate's comments on Benjamin's thesis XVII, which opposes the historian who reconstructs the past to the memory that reconstructs its meaning. Reyes Mate says, taking Benjamin's teaching for the Spanish case:

> One cannot understand the reality called Spain without mending the fracture. And that mending begins with a specific assessment of the fracture, not subsumable or dissolvable in a transcendent concept of Spain, in which what has been expelled is irrelevant. The amputated does not heal with an interpretation in which the specific, traumatic event is subsumed in the logic of the whole. Once the expulsion has taken place, the explanation of the whole has to be made from the particularity of the expulsion. Instead of subsuming the particular into the whole, the whole must be judged from the particular. The marginal becomes a privileged observatory of the process as a whole. To point out this new situation of a fact charged with unforeseen universalist responsibilities.
> *(Reyes Mate, 2006, p. 266)*

Therefore, to "seize hold of a memory as it flashes in a moment of danger" could perhaps mean reconstructing an identity (individual, intersubjective, socio-historical) from the traumatic marks of what could not be, from the emptiness left by annihilation, terror and absence. This narrative identity could be founded on and structured around the trauma itself in an attempt to confront the various repressions, denials and repetition-compulsions resulting from the traumatic event and/or its consequences.

In his concept of narrative identity, Ricœur also discusses the relationship between the historical and the psychoanalytic. More precisely, he argues:

> Psychoanalytic experience throws into relief the role of the narrative component in what are usually called "case histories." It is in the work of the analysand, which by the way Freud called "working-through" (*Durcharbeitung*), that this role can be grasped. It is further justified by the very goal of the whole process of the cure, which is to substitute for the bits and pieces of stories that are unintelligible as well as unbearable, a coherent and acceptable story, in which the analysand can recognize his or her self-constancy. In this regard, psychoanalysis constitutes a particularly instructive laboratory for a properly philosophical inquiry into the notion of narrative identity. In it, we can see how the story of a life comes to be constituted through a series of rectifications applied to previous narratives, just as the history of a people, or a collectivity, or an institution proceeds from the series of corrections that new historians bring to their predecessors' descriptions and explanations, and, step by step, to the legends that preceded this genuinely historiographical work. As has been said, history always proceeds from history.
> *(Ricœur, 1984–1988, Volume 3, p. 247)*

The concept of narrative identity, then, helps overcome the inconsistency between time and identity and allows us to understand both the evolutionary purpose of memory as a system designed for action and its significance for historians. This does not mean that narrative identity is a stable and reified process in time. On the contrary, Ricœur himself recognizes that its boundaries are complex and unstable, and that the ultimate limit of identity, as Benjamin had already pointed out, is ethical. Thus, Ricœur concludes on this subject:

> In the first place, narrative identity is not a stable and seamless identity. Just as it is possible to compose several plots on the subject of the same incidents (which, thus, should not really be called the same events), so it is always possible to weave different, even opposed, plots about our lives. [...] In this sense, narrative identity continues to make and unmake itself, and the question of trust that Jesus posed to his disciples – Who do you say that I am? – is one that each of us can pose concerning ourself, with the same perplexity that the disciples questioned by Jesus felt. [...] So narrative identity is not equivalent to true self-constancy except through this decisive moment, which makes ethical responsibility the highest factor in self-constancy. Levinas's well-known analysis of promise-keeping and, in a way, his whole work bear witness to this. The plea that the theory of narrative can always oppose to ethics' claim to be the sole judge of the constitution of subjectivity would be to recall that narrativity is not denuded of every normative, evaluative, or prescriptive dimension. The theory of reading has warned us that the strategy of persuasion undertaken by the narrator is aimed at imposing on the reader a vision of the world that is never ethically neutral, but that rather implicitly or explicitly induces a new evaluation of the world and of the reader as well. In this sense, narrative already belongs to the ethical field in virtue of its claim – inseparable from its narration – to ethical justice.
>
> *(Ricœur, 1984–1988, Volume 3, p. 247)*

Memory, then, is a creative act. It exists to guide present actions, not to fixate us in the past. At the same time, it gives us a sense of continuity in time, insofar as it allows us to construct a personal, inter-subjective and socio-historical identity. It weaves the fragments of the past into diverse narratives which are ultimately ethical in nature. These constitute us as individuals, as groups, as peoples and as humanity.

It remains to examine the various narrative approaches to experiences of genocide. The purpose of this will be to understand what type of identity each narrative tends to build, whether it encourages us to own or disown the past, and to work through trauma. In each case, we also need to understand how historical sufferings have been assimilated, and what ethical premises underlie the narrative identities that emerge from different conceptualizations of history. Law is one of the few performative discourses that produces immediate effects, so we will also need to know how legal decisions affect these narrative structures.

The next chapter will go to the heart of the hypothesis contained in the first volume of this trilogy: *that memory processes, identity formation and working through trauma are all affected by the different ways that state crimes have been represented.*

Notes

1 Among the many authors who have written about this topic are Carlo Guinzburg, Hayden White, Dominick LaCapra, Berel Lang, Enzo Traverso and Paul Ricœur.
2 Original translator's note: "The Hegelian term "aufheben" in its threefold meaning: to preserve, to elevate and to cancel.
3 During the Rwandan genocide, for example, one euphemism for murder heard repeatedly in directives issued on the Hutu extremist RTLM radio was that of "clearing" the Tutsi from the land.

References

Assmann, J. (2006). *Religion and cultural memory: Ten studies.* Rodney Livingstone, trans. Stanford University Press.
Bartlett, F. C. (1932). *Remembering: A study in experimental and social psychology.* Cambridge University Press.
Benjamin, W. (1969). *Illuminations* (Harry Zohn, Trans., with an introduction by Hannah Arendt, Ed.). Schocken Books.
Bergson, H. (1944) [1911]. *Creative evolution* (Arthur Mitchell, authorized Trans.). The Modern Library.
Bergson, H. (1919). *Matter and memory* (Nancy Margaret Paul & W. Scott Palmer, authorized Trans.), 5th ed. George Allen & Unwin Ltd.
Bosch, T. E. (2016). Memory Studies, A brief concept paper. (Working Paper). *MeCoDEM*, ISSN 2057-4002. p. 5. https://eprints.whiterose.ac.uk/117289/1/Bosch%20 2016_Memory%20Studies.pdf
Cassel, J. C., Cassel, D., & Manning, L. (2013). From Augustine of Hippo's memory systems to our modern taxonomy in cognitive psychology and neuroscience of memory: A 16-century map of intuition before light of evidence. *Behavioral Sciences*, 3, 21–41. https://doi.org/10.3390/bs3010021
Edelman, G. M., & Tononi, G. (2000). *A universe of consciousness: How matter becomes imagination.* Basic Books.
Feierstein, D. (2000). *Seis estudios sobre genocidio. Análisis de las relaciones sociales: otredad, exclusion, exterminio.* EUDEBA.
Feierstein, D. (2014). *Genocide as social practice. Reorganizing society under Nazism and Argentina's military juntas.* Rutgers University Press. (Spanish original version: *El genocidio como práctica social: entre el nazismo y la experiencia argentina*, Buenos Aires, FCE, 2007.)
Friedländer, S. (Ed.) (1992). Probing the limits of representation. In *Nazism and the final solution.* Harvard University Press.

Halbwachs, M. (1992). *On collective memory* (Lewis A. Coser, Ed., Trans., with an introduction.). University of Chicago Press.

LaCapra, D. (1998). *History and memory after Auschwitz*. Cornell University Press.

Moses, A. D. (2011). Genocide and the terror of history. *Parallax, 17*(4), 90–108. https://doi.org/10.1080/13534645.2011.605583

Pollak, M. (1989). Memória, Esquecimento, Silêncio [Memory, forgetting, silence]. *Revista Estudos Históricos, 2,* 3–15.

Prado-Alcala, R. A., & Quirarte, G. L. (2007). The consolidation of memory, one century on [article in Spanish]. *Revista De Neurología, 45*(5), 284–292. https://www.researchgate.net/publication/5965772_The_consolidation_of_memory_one_century_on

Reyes Mate, M. (2006). Medianoche de la historia. *Comentarios a las tesis de Walter Benjamin "Sobre el concepto de Historia.* Trotta.

Ricœur, P. (1984–1988). *Time and narrative* (Kathleen McLaughlin & David Pellauer, Trans.). University of Chicago Press.

Ricœur, P. (1991). *Life in quest of narrative in: From text to action: Essays in Hermeneutics II* (Kathleen Blamey & John B. Thompson, Trans.). Northwestern University Press.

Ricoeur, P. (2004). *Memory, history, forgetting* (Kathleen Blamey & David Pellauer, Trans.). University of Chicago Press.

White, H. (1973). *Metahistory: The historical imagination in nineteenth-century Europe.* Johns Hopkins University Press.

Winocur, G., & Moscovitch, M. (2011). Memory transformation and systems consolidation. *Journal of the International Neuropsychological Society, 17*(5), 766–780. https://doi.org/10.1017/S1355617711000683

4
HOW CONCEPTS AND REPRESENTATIONS SHAPE IDENTITY

Research in various fields, including neuroscience, psychoanalysis, social psychology, social sciences, history and philosophy, suggests that the way in which state crimes are described can impact the identity of survivors and their ability to process trauma. At the social level, this process can be facilitated through the legal system and the pursuit of justice for the perpetrators. However, it is not just about punishment, but also about how the crimes are defined – whether as war crimes, crimes against humanity or genocide. This chapter examines the various legal, historical and sociological descriptions of state crimes and their potential to empower victims.

One of the key points highlighted in previous chapters was the need for dialogue between disciplines. Often, each field of study operates within its own set of principles and therefore exaggerates disagreements with others on how the law should address past traumatic events. However, the law has the ability to facilitate resolution and healing through its ability to serve as a forum for addressing these issues. Judicial decisions, including sentences, often become widely accepted truths and narratives that hold more weight than those formed elsewhere. In addition to the symbolic impact of legal proceedings, there are also tangible consequences for those involved, including punishment for the guilty and compensation for victims for the harm they have suffered (Feierstein, 2015a).

Because today we entrust judges with creating state-approved discourses, the judicial system plays dual roles in creating truth and punishing wrongdoing. Its discourses are widely implemented by various policymakers and social actors, regardless of personal opinions or the critiques of social scientists, philosophers or historians regarding their possibly illusory or fictional nature. It is important to remember that a judge's ruling remains in force, even

DOI: 10.4324/9781003336464-5

if it is subjected to critical discourse analysis. This should also be understood by jurists who claim that representations in social sciences do not affect legal discourse in any way.

This chapter will examine the disagreement on how to classify the human rights abuses that occurred in Argentina during the 1970s and 1980s, with a focus on the National Security Doctrine implemented in Latin America. The analysis is also relevant to other instances of mass violence, including the genocide committed by the Ittihadists against the Armenian, Assyrians and Greeks in Turkey; genocide committed by the Nazis against the Jews, Roma, homosexuals, Jehova's Witnesses, political dissidents, handicapped among other groups; the Rwandan genocide or the genocidal cases in the Former Yugoslavia, Bangladesh, Cambodia, Sri Lanka and Myanmar. It is important to consider these issues within their historical context in order to fully understand the complexities and nuances involved.

It is also important to note that legal concepts are not all-powerful, and do not automatically open every door. They are simply abbreviated versions of different stories that can provide different opportunities for resolution. Additionally, legal concepts are specific forms of representation, which are based on history. Therefore, when examining the meanings of terms like genocide, war, state terrorism or crimes against humanity, it is necessary to consider how these concepts are used within each specific context. In this case, I will be analyzing the context of Argentina, particularly during the 1970s.

This, then, is the fundamental objective of the first volume of the trilogy. The next volume (volume 2) will delve deeper into the logic of the legal system, including the rules governing legal sentencing and other relevant factors. Consequently, these topics will not be covered in great detail in volume 1. Instead, we will focus on how these elements can create sets of representations that may become widely accepted as true within a given society. The final book, volume 3 titled *Responsibilities*, will explore the *impacts* of different sets of representations and value judgements on social practices.

Memory as a process: The search for meaning and coherence

As we saw in the first chapter, one of neuroscience's most significant discoveries in the past 30 years is that memory is not stored at a specific location in the brain. Instead, different types of memories are stored in different regions of the brain that are interconnected. According to philosophers like Bergson and Freud, all memory is a reconstruction of various sensations, perceptions, learned responses, motor routines and so on. These can be classified into different categories such as semantic, episodic and procedural memory. Semantic memory contains general knowledge about the world, such as the fact that bicycles have two wheels, pedals and handlebars. It thus provides the memory necessary to use language. Episodic memory allows us to recall specific events from our personal past, like receiving our first bike. Procedural memory includes skills like the ability to ride a bike (Tulving, 1972). However, even episodic memories are actually a collection of disordered and fragmentary experiences that are only given meaning through a narrative.

Memory, then, is not simply a process of reproducing past events, but rather a process of creating new experiences and understandings through the integration of old and new information. This process of creation occurs within consciousness, even when unconscious factors may influence our thoughts and behaviors. As Edelman and Tononi have noted: "In higher organisms every act of perception is, to some extent, an act of creation, and every act of memory is, to some extent, an act of imagination" (Edelman & Tononi, 2000, p. 27).

The search for meaning lies at the heart of all the reconstructions we call "memory." For this reason, Edelman and Tononi also suggested that "consciousness does not tolerate breaks of coherence" (Edelman & Tononi, 2000, p. 27) and that "the drive towards integration is so strong that one often does not perceive a void where, in reality, there is a horrendous abyss" (Edelman & Tononi, 2000, p. 29). As was also pointed out in the first chapter: "Apparently, the feeling of an absence is far less tolerable than the absence of a feeling" (Edelman & Tononi, 2000, p. 29).

But that is not all. The search for meaning is linked to action, as Freud and Bergson recognized and as discussed in Chapters 2 and 3. This connection is formed through the creation of a "scene," which is a structured series of isolated memories. This process is driven by the current need for action, even when that need is not consciously recognized. In some cases, this need may be driven by what Freud called "repetition compulsion" – the reenactment of unprocessed trauma, often through recurrent dreams.

Halbwachs and Bartlett, among others, have shown that the search for meaning in memory is a social process that occurs within the context of relationships with others. This can involve external relationships with other people or internal relationships with our own memories of others. All memory is thus shaped by the interactions and experiences we have with others, as well as by the collective memories of those who came before us. Individual memories are not isolated, but rather are constructed within the broader context of social and historical influences.

Benjamin emphasizes that history can be presented in different ways: the historicist version of the victors versus the memories that *flash in the moment of danger* of the oppressed. Ricœur suggests that such memories are also connected to the creation of identity in the present, as the stories we tell about *ourselves* and *others* are influenced by historical reality.

The legal concepts that are used to understand and address state crimes in Argentina between 1974 and 1983 – the so-called process of national reorganization – shape our understanding of past events and provide a foundation for present action. The ways in which we depict and interpret these events, as well as the legal concepts that condense them, emerge from a search for social meaning. Moreover, these representations play a crucial role in enabling society to rebuild and redefine its identities after such a traumatic period. However, this process is always vulnerable to *desensitization*, a coping mechanism that can manifest at both the physiological and psychological levels, as well as through ideologies of meaninglessness (as discussed in Chapter 2).

The main issue in discussing and understanding massive state violence in Argentina and elsewhere, I will argue, is *not* determining which of the possible descriptions is the "truest" or most accurate. In the case of Argentina, all the various narratives and descriptions contain some element of truth. Unlike other historical cases, denialist or minimizing narratives have only gained strength in Argentina since 2013. These versions will not be considered in this analysis (Feierstein, 2018).

The accuracy of a report on state crimes, such as torture, murder, disappearances, child abduction, rape and others, depends on whether these crimes were actually committed. However, the relevance of a legal or historical-sociological concept is not only based on the occurrence of events, but also on the way these are understood and whether a society accepts both the facts and their interpretation.

The understanding, analysis and critique of concepts used to describe experience should be based on their ability to create various interpretations in the process of reflecting on experience and also on how they shape the construction of identities.[1]

The distinction between concepts and facts has not been thoroughly examined, particularly in regard to how concepts are used to analyze historical experiences. It is important to understand that concepts are not facts, although they are often mistaken for such by social scientists and legal scholars. Instead, concepts are narrative and symbolic constructs that *give meaning to facts*. Therefore, determining whether or not there was a war, crimes against humanity or genocide in Argentina cannot be based solely on factual evidence (such as the number of casualties or incidents of violence). It also depends on how each of the concepts is defined and the extent to which society considers that they are appropriate.

When concepts are clearly and specifically tied to visible phenomena and there is an agreement about their meaning, they can be considered "observable." For example, we all understand what a homicide is and it refers to a specific type of action (a living body becomes lifeless due to a human action). There have been similar efforts to define and agree upon the concepts of torture, rape or forced disappearance, although there is still debate about their boundaries and whether certain actions should be included within these concepts. It is clear that debates about how to define these concepts (torture, rape, forced disappearance) have significant political consequences and impact not only the past but also the present and future of the societies in which they occur. Consensus can only be reached when a definition is either clearly and forcefully established or has achieved such widespread acceptance that it is not questioned.

Concepts like war crimes, genocide and crimes against humanity are less easy to apply than concepts like murder, torture and rape. Because of their novelty and complexity, they still have no formal and consensus-based definition as observables. As a result, they are still interpreted differently based on the observables they attempt to describe.

Consequently, the process of turning facts or concepts into something that can be observed cannot be solely addressed by considering their accuracy. Even when people hold different understandings of concepts or use them differently, they may still recognize the same factual truths and identify the same observables, but interpret them differently and conceptually. To truly understand this process, it is necessary to delve deeper and examine the effects and consequences that different narratives, conceptualizations and models of representation can have on the way we experience and understand the world.

Reviewing conceptual understandings of the Argentinean case

The systematic and wide-scale human rights violations that occurred in Argentina during the 1970s and 1980s have been represented in many ways. However, these representations can be grouped around four main concepts used to describe the events: war, genocide, crimes against humanity and state terrorism. Crimes against humanity is often considered to be the legal formulation of the sociological concept of state terrorism although there are differences between them as we shall see.[2]

Although these categories have some overlap, they are distinct and can be distinguished from one another based on the legal or historical-sociological focus of the narrative. These modes of representation have had various expressions and have played different roles in shaping public understanding of the events.

This does not imply that the various labels are exclusive or contradictory. On the contrary, some authors use two or even three categories simultaneously.[3] However, the specific focus placed on one or another creates different patterns of understanding of Argentine history. It also impacts the symbolic effects of judgments and verdicts and consequently the ability of the immediate victims and society at large to work through trauma.

Three of the concepts involved in these representations – genocide, crimes against humanity and state terrorism – still compete for meaning and dominance. The fourth concept – war – has been used by those responsible for crimes as a means to legitimize their actions and seek acquittal for their defendants. It is true, nevertheless, that some survivors of left-wing insurgent organizations and some theorists argue that the term "civil war" is a fair and accurate description of the events. However, this attempt to separate conceptual analysis and the legal consequences of these definitions is not without difficulties, as there is a close connection between the two levels in the ways in which these different forms of representation are argued and the consequences that result from them.

To begin with, we will examine the ways in which each of the three main types of representation (war, genocide, crimes against humanity) organizes information into a narrative structure. Once we have done this, we will then look at how these different structures impact our understanding of the information at various levels of analysis.

War

The discourse of war has been expressed in very different ways in Argentina, with some approaches being diametrically opposed in political and ideological terms. Despite being a common-sense notion during the 1970s, it was heavily discredited in the aftermath of the dictatorship. Currently, it is only held by a small minority in Argentina, including those sympathetic to the perpetrators, some survivors of left-wing armed groups and a few academic circles.[4] Moreover, the perspectives on war in Argentina are highly divergent, with different groups using adjectives such as "anti-subversive," "dirty," "revolutionary," "counter-revolutionary," "counter-insurgency" or "civilian," among others. However, it is interesting to note that this narrow view is still prevalent in English-language works on Argentina, which tend to summarize the entire experience under the umbrella term "dirty war."

The aim here is not to align different perspectives on war from ideological, theoretical and moral-ethical viewpoints, as each group has a different understanding of the concept of war and uses it for different purposes. However, it is worth noting that the interpretation of events as war can have common effects on the construction of historical meaning, its impact on the present and the formation of collective identities. This is regardless of the political nature of different discourses on war, the intentions of their creators or their moral-ethical consequences.

Discourses on war often focus on the political and social upheaval that took place in the country at the end of the 1960s. According to the military and their allies, this unrest represented a threat to the Argentine nation, which they attributed to foreign influences such as communism, atheism and Freemasonry. On the other hand, armed left-wing organizations, notably the (Peronist) Montoneros and the (Marxist) Ejército Revolucionario del Pueblo (Revolutionary People´s Army), saw themselves as *armies*. For them, *war* was a reaction by the ruling class to the radicalization of the popular sectors and the emergence of militarized Peronist and Marxist groups. They argued that the war was a counterrevolutionary attempt to prevent the development of a socialist project in Argentina, a project fueled by the Peronist resistance and the successes of the Cuban Revolution and other insurrectionary movements.

For other more academic authors such as Juan Carlos Marín (1996), "civil war" is a split within society between the ruling bloc and the revolutionary bloc, resulting in a shift in the balance of power from a primarily political stage to a political-military stage, according to Antonio Gramsci's classification. Some perspectives on civil war emphasize the covert nature of the conflict as a means of creating a divide between armed organizations and the popular movement. These perspectives focus on the "casualties" (wounded, killed, kidnapped) that occurred in the spaces where social movements and left-wing armed organizations intersected, providing valuable insight into the impact of the past.

The concept of "dirty war" used by the perpetrators refers to a type of conflict characterized by covert operations and targeted repression against the civilian population, rather than open, conventional warfare between military forces on a battlefield.[5] These types of conflicts often involved irregular or guerrilla forces, and the perpetrators used tactics such as clandestine operations and police repression to try to undermine the support of the population for these movements, by "depriving the fish of water." This type of warfare is often associated with the French counterinsurgency doctrine, which was developed during the wars in Indochina and Algeria and later disseminated to other countries by the United States through the School of the Americas. This doctrine emphasizes the importance of targeting the civilian population in order to weaken the support for the enemy, rather than engaging in direct, open combat with the enemy's military forces.

Now, within the existing criminal justice system, the existence of a "dirty" war would only legitimize the prosecution of the "excesses" and "errors" to which it gave rise, Obviously, the perpetrators of these actions do not recognize that these took place. Some victims, however, have referred to the events as a war and described these "excesses" or "mistakes" as potential war crimes, including, for example:

a Violating the laws of war by committing shooting, abducting, raping and torturing members of the enemy army who are unable to defend themselves;
b Abducting, torturing, looting, raping and/or killing civilians who are not directly participating in hostilities;
c Suppressing the identity of children of enemy combatants, whether they were abducted with their parents or born in captivity, or of civilians not participating directly in hostilities; and
d Using disproportionate force by continuing operations after the enemy force has been definitively defeated, turning the war into a campaign of annihilation, which allows some authors to equate this concept of civil war with genocide.

The government of President Alfonsín, the report of the National Commission on the Disappearance of Persons (CONADEP) and the proceedings in the Trial of the Military Juntas in 1985 rejected the notion that there had been a war in Argentina. However, the predominant view, later termed by the left as the "theory of the two demons," argued that the persecution of certain individuals was justified because they were part of left-wing armed groups that posed a threat to the state. Thus, the focus was placed on the alleged errors and excesses in the use of state force, rather than on the legitimacy of the persecution itself.

Clearly, not all discourses accept that war crimes were committed or – if they were – that they should be prosecuted. There are also significant differences in how these crimes are categorized in different discussions about war. Nevertheless, despite these different and even conflicting evaluations, there are some fundamental themes that are shared by these discourses. These themes include:

1 There were two main groups involved in the conflict: one group, which can be described as "the nation," "the legal forces," "the Argentine army," or "the hegemonic bloc," "the regime," or "the counter-revolutionary forces" and the other group, which can be referred to as "the subversion," "the international communist aggression," "the popular camp" or "the revolutionary forces." Both groups were social forces with political and military wings, although they differed significantly in terms of their positive or negative impact on the Argentine nation.
2 That the beginning of hostilities can be explained by the growing radicalization of political struggles in Argentina – whether or not this radicalization includes the militarization of left-wing forces. Therefore, it was a "defensive" war, regardless of what it was intended to defend (the nation, institutions, the dominant order or oligarchic power).
3 The terror that affected Argentine society was a "reaction" to events that occurred before the decision to use terror was made.

Theories of war can differ significantly based on their analysis of this defensive "reaction," and this leads to different consequences:

a Those who support the idea of military action argue that it was necessary to address the threat posed by rebel factions through the "dirty war," which was a result of the threat posed by these groups to the nation.
b According to the democratist perspective that emerged in the 1980s and led to the Trial of the Military Juntas, the main problem with the last dictatorship was the disproportionate response to the perceived threat, as well as the involvement of innocent civilians who had no connection to the conflict (these issues are addressed in the prologue to the *Nunca Más*

Report, although the report denies the classification of the events as a war and instead frames them as common crimes committed by a terrorist state).

c Finally, those who support the idea of a "popular struggle" claim that the harsh response was necessary in order to teach Argentine society a "lesson" and prevent the resurgence of political radicalization or the revival of the revolutionary project through terror. This terror was part of a "counter-revolutionary" policy.

Despite significant differences, a common theme can be identified in the confrontation between two social forces, which escalates to a military stage. This confrontation is often explained as the result of an initial action of political-military radicalization that leads to a defensive reaction and ultimately a repressive process.

In the following sections, we will examine other narrative models and evaluate their impact on the interpretation of the past in the present and their potential for healing.

Genocide

The concept of genocide was first introduced in a legal document by Eduardo Luis Duhalde in his analysis of the events that occurred during Argentina's military dictatorship as a denounce from the exile through the association CADHU (Comisión Argentina de Derechos Humanos, Argentine Commission on Human Rights), established in February 1976 in different countries in Europe by Argentine exiled.[6] Later, Eduardo Barcesat, lawyer for the Israel and Fernández Meijide families, argued that the military trials initiated in 1985 should be conducted under the accusation of genocide, as this classification would allow for a better understanding of the systematic nature of the plan behind the individual crimes. Barcesat believed that using the classification of genocide would also show a stricter adherence to the principle of legality, as Argentina had ratified the Convention on the Prevention and Punishment of the Crime of Genocide before the events in question. However, this classification was rejected by the Federal Court in charge of case 13/84, as well as by President Alfonsín's legal advisors, and even by the majority of the plaintiffs at the time. In 1998, Alfredo Astiz was indicted for the apology of the crime of genocide, setting a precedent that was not followed until the 2006 sentence of the Federal Oral Court No. 1 of La Plata in the case against Miguel Osvaldo Etchecolatz.

It is worth noting that many human rights organizations, including the Permanent Assembly for Human Rights, Mothers of Plaza de Mayo, Grandmothers of Plaza de Mayo, Association of Former Disappeared Detainees and even some sectors of HIJOS (the acronym in Spanish for "Children for

Identity and Justice Against Forgetting and Silence"), consistently and increasingly used the term genocide in the 1980s and 1990s. This use of the term can also be traced back to a reference to the "genocidal magnitude" of the crimes committed by the military dictatorship in Rodolfo Walsh's Open Letter to the Military Junta, which was written in March 1977 before he was assassinated by the military.

The concept of genocide has been used in the work of historians like Luis Alberto Romero (1994), although he later regretted it, jurists like Mirta Mántaras (2005), and research teams at the University of Buenos Aires and the National University of Tres de Febrero since the 1990s and early 21st century (Feierstein, 1997, 2000, 2005, 2014). These works have been referenced by numerous courts in Argentina and around the world in discussions and decisions regarding the legal classification of genocide.

The concept of genocide is used in various discourses, each of which has its own nuances. However, these discourses also have common elements in their meaning, as well as in their ideological and political implications. Here we are not so much concerned with internal differences within each classification or narrative structure, as with the fundamental differences between the four main representations of the events: war, genocide, crimes against humanity and state terrorism.

Characterizing the events as genocide reflects a larger project in which the use of terror and its widespread impact on society is a fundamental aspect of the practice, rather than an unusual excess or derivative of it. To claim that Argentina experienced a genocide implies that there was a plan for social and national reorganization, which aimed to destroy social relations based on autonomy and cooperation by killing a significant portion of society (significant in numbers or influence) and that then attempts to create new social relations and identity models through terror (Feierstein, 2014, p. 35).

In relation to the elements analyzed in the previous paragraph, it can be argued:

1 The victims of the terror – a terror imposed through torture chambers, concentration camps and "disappearances" – cannot be divided into "central" vs. "accessory", or "guilty" vs. "innocent," because terror was aimed at the whole of society, including the perpetrators and their families. The definition of the target to be persecuted, the "subversive delinquent," was intentionally ambiguous and could include "subversives, accomplices, sympathizers, the indifferent and the timid," according to the perpetrators themselves.[7] This means that terror sought to produce effects on all of society. It was not just "excessive" repression of armed left-wing groups, but rather a more radical and profound practice targeted at the entire Argentine national group, not just its radicalized or militarized fractions.

2 The actions were not initiated by previous radicalization leading to a reaction, but rather by the careful and persistent creation of a project to reorganize society through terrorism. This project was justified by the "fight against subversion," but it was actually designed before there were armed left-wing organizations in Argentina or popular sectors became radicalized. As a continental project expressed in the National Security Doctrine, it was autonomous and independent of the strength of the insurgent organizations or the perceived threat of a revolutionary project. This "reorganizing" project is evident in its implementation in situations of civil war (such as El Salvador), in situations where there were insurgent forces without the ability to openly engage in military combat (such as Guatemala or Argentina), and even in situations where there were almost no actions by the armed left that challenged the state apparatus (such as Chile or Bolivia).

3 This action in question was, therefore, not a "defensive" or "reactionary" measure, but rather an "offensive" one that sought to transform social relations based on reciprocity and cooperation into relations based on individualism and a lack of responsibility. It was a project that was relatively independent from the extent to which guerrilla activity was present in the region and was driven by the desire to use the concentration camp system and the terror it generated as a means of transforming social relations. Informing on others was presumably one of the behaviors encouraged in order to take advantage of the damaging and long-lasting effects of this practice in breaking down and transforming social bonds, identities, and subjectivities.

It is worth noting that this unique way of understanding and structuring the concept of genocide has not been common in other historical cases. The uniqueness of how the concept is used in Argentina is that it is separated from the binary character that often accompanies the vision of genocide as a racial or tribal conflict. Thus, the concept has become more analytical over time, first implicitly and not entirely consciously. In contrast, the use of the concept of genocide in many works about the case of Guatemala often prioritizes an understanding of the conflict in terms of the indigenization of the victims and its subsequent depoliticization, a phenomenon also seen in many views of Nazism but not present in the application of the concept to the Argentine case.

State terrorism

The concept of the "terrorist state" was first introduced by Eduardo Duhalde in a notable work that has left a lasting impact on Argentina's collective memory (Duhalde, 1999). Duhalde linked this concept with that of genocide, but the term "state terrorism" was later adopted by many historians, social scientists, and even some human rights organizations, judges, prosecutors and plaintiffs to differentiate themselves from those who used the term genocide to describe what had taken place. This led to significant differences in the interpretation of the events, many of which are not addressed in Duhalde's original work.[8]

In this work, Duhalde examines the role of secret practices, the purpose of terror, and the distinction between "measures of exception" and "state of exception," making it an essential reference for analyzing this period. The "dual" structure of state functioning is one of the key factors in understanding how modern states systematically annihilate populations. Another important concept in the text is that the main goal of a terrorist state is not to "militarize" society, but rather to "disarticulate" it. From this perspective, the events described can be seen as the destruction and reformation of social relations, a central aspect of what I have characterized as a "reorganizing genocide" (Feierstein, 2014). In some cases, the author even goes so far as to list specific behaviors, such as encouraging denunciation, undermining solidarity and fostering individualism, as tactics employed by this type of state.

Just as many works on Nazism and the Genocide Convention "depoliticized" genocide as a way of understanding the specific nature of Nazi persecution, the notion of a "state terrorism" underwent a similar redefinition. It was viewed as a practical strategy employed by the state, and thus as the primary source of the "violations" in question. This perspective was significantly different from Duhalde's and obscured the connection between torture and the social-economic order to which torture was functional, a connection authors like Duhalde sought to shed light on.[9]

In many works and perspectives that prioritize the concept of a terrorist state and/or link it to the legal category of "crimes against humanity," Duhalde's concept is stripped of its controversial origins. It is diluted in the description of an operational mode of a military dictatorship that seized constitutional power. These texts have become relatively dominant in the field of defining the period as a "terrorist state," overshadowing Duhalde's work and presenting a vision whose main points could be characterized as follows.

In terms of the identity of those involved in the conflict, these texts contrast the "terrorist state" on the one hand and the "group of citizens" on the other. However, the main difference with the concept of genocide is that these texts do not view the victims as members of a "national group" (which is why they deny the category of genocide), but rather as politicized individuals who suffered the violation of their individual rights (such as the right to life, integrity, security and well-being) and were persecuted. These victims supposedly differ from those in a genocidal process in that their identity can be analyzed as "chosen" or "voluntary," as opposed to an "involuntary" or essential ethnic or national identity.[10]

Now, it is important to point out the following. Distinctions between voluntary and involuntary or stable and unstable identities assume the existence of unchanging identities (for example, ethnic or national) and the supposed ability of the researcher to distinguish them. However, when we examine the foundations of this perspective and its philosophical and sociological consequences in terms of identity construction, we find that this process is not supported.[11]

In the previous chapter, it was noted that all identity is a narrative construction, meaning that instability and change are inherent in its very existence. Because identity is a fragile unity that seeks to unite different histories and activities over time, it is clear that it cannot be static or fixed, regardless of whether it is ethnic, religious or political. Additionally, since identity involves both conscious and unconscious elements, the notion that it is voluntary becomes questionable, as it is difficult to think of unconscious elements being chosen freely. Ultimately, the discussion about how to define the victims leads to the fundamental legal distinction between crimes against humanity (indiscriminate actions against civilian populations) and genocide (discriminatory actions against specific groups of the population).

The terrorist state in Argentina can be understood as a specific form of genocidal practice against the Argentine national group, as initially proposed by Duhalde. However, many people believe that the concept of a terrorist state or crimes against humanity should only refer to violations of citizens' rights by the state, rather than focusing on the suffering of specific groups. This approach emphasizes the individual rights of citizens who have been harmed by state actions such as kidnapping, torture, rape, murder and the suppression of identity.

It is important to note that the mention of "the political" as being ideological, focused on party involvement or "convictions," hides the economic foundation of the campaigns of destruction in the Southern Cone. This foundation is evident in the representations of war and genocide, and has been manifested in different cases as *class war, shock doctrine* or *restructuring genocide*.

In terms of how actions were initiated, those who speak of state terrorism do not have a consistent discourse. Some argue that state terrorism was a response to political radicalization, although it was a totally disproportionate and inappropriate response, as the CONADEP report *"Never Again"* also stated. Others, however, see state terrorism as an independent project, more in line with the concept of genocide, as argued by Duhalde and the second phase of Luis Alberto Romero's work. In contrast, the other two explanatory modes do have a shared discourse.

In conclusion, there is often more agreement on the ideological implications of different versions of the "terrorist state" as compared to "war." There are still differing explanations for how the conflict began and where the decision to implement terrorist actions originated. However, all these explanations categorize the victims similarly, and it is this fact that distinguishes the perspective of "state terrorism" from the perspectives of war or genocide.

It is important to consider that in many instances, crimes against humanity are classified as such for "legal and technical" reasons rather than out of a genuine understanding of the events in question. In some cases, this classification is used to portray the victims as "political groups" rather than individuals who have been targeted by the state's punitive power. This classification ignores the fundamental principle underlying the concept of genocide, which is *not* to treat the victims and their suffering as isolated and individual cases.

It would be interesting to apply these frameworks of analysis to other historical events where the dominance of one perspective is particularly clear. For example, in Spain, there was undeniably a civil war – with open warfare and more or less professional armies, which did not exist in Argentina. This made it impossible for alternative, more nuanced interpretations such as genocide to emerge, both during the civil war and throughout the Franco regime which followed. Nevertheless, both involved significantly more summary executions and torture than were committed in Argentina.

It is uncommon to consider the extent to which the inability to achieve justice and healing in the Spanish case is connected to a militaristic us-and-them perspective. This perspective prevents us from examining how terror impacted Spanish society as a whole and the responsibilities that resulted from it. For instance, there has been almost no discussion on the abduction of minors in Spain, in contrast to the attention given to the Grandmothers of Plaza de Mayo in their fight to recover kidnapped children in Argentina. This is surprising given that the phenomenon was much less prevalent in Argentina, with an estimated 500 cases as compared to Spain, where more than 30,000 children were abducted in a network involving the active participation of the Spanish Catholic Church.

Something similar has happened in Colombia with the notion of "armed conflict," which has obscured the recognition of the genocidal nature of certain events, presenting them instead as part of a war. This has been a hindrance, despite the fact that in recent years there has been significant progress in acknowledging this in Colombia, unlike in Spain.

The link between memory and the present: We live in a "remembered present"

In this section, we will examine the implications of the three main ways of describing Argentina's traumatic past – war, genocide and state terrorism (or crimes against humanity as its legal form). We will consider how they allow for the consequences of terror to be addressed, whether they tend to

How concepts and representations shape identity

encourage us to own the past or otherwise, and whether they offer opportunities for healing. We will do this by analyzing six different areas:

a how the victims are defined;
b the meaning assigned to the past;
c the types of analogies and comparisons each label gives rise to;
d how the social consequences of terror are evaluated;
e the actions proposed or assumed to be necessary for healing and/or to prevent a repetition of the terror; and
f intergenerational transmission (including mourning) and the ways in which each form of representation helps us to own the past or not.

It is worth noting that in many cases, these areas overlap and combine in more complex explanations that incorporate two or three of the main perspectives.

How the victims are defined

We have already mentioned some of the different ways of thinking about the victims' implicit in the concepts of war, genocide, crimes against humanity and state terrorism. Including a legal perspective can also make a valuable contribution to our analysis. Argentine law uses the term "passive subjects" where English would say the "victims" of a crime. Arguably, "passive subject of the crime" emphasizes for Spanish speakers that there are degrees of victimhood. Recent work in Canada on victimology identifies categories of victims based on emotional or psychological proximity to the victimization: (1) direct victims, (2) indirect victims, (3) secondary victims and (4) tertiary victims. Direct victims are people who are unlawfully killed, disappeared, tortured and so on. Indirect victims are people such as family members and friends who have close ties to a direct victim. Secondary victims are persons who have witnessed the victimization. Tertiary victims refer to community members. All of these different groups of victims can suffer trauma and other consequences as a result of their experiences (Wemmers, 2021). This is important when thinking about the effects of different narratives on the healing process.

As regards the question of victimhood, the three narratives (war, genocide and state terrorism) could be summarized as follows:

1 In the context of war theories, those who can be considered as deserving justice are the innocent individuals who were not involved in the conflict and suffered from state terrorism. This perspective is shared by various theories of war and the theories of "the two demons," which argue that Argentina experienced both extreme left-wing and extreme right-wing

terrorism. This viewpoint can be found in numerous works, including the prologue written by Ernesto Sábato for the "Informe Nunca Más" report produced by the CONADEP in 1984.

Those who consider themselves combatants in a war often do not see themselves as victims or "affected" individuals, and may not even view the events as crimes. However, for those who feel or consider themselves defeated in the war, the terror and extermination inflicted by the regime is a further demonstration of the inhumane actions of one side, which only reinforces the legitimacy of the struggle they engaged in and may lead to a pursuit of legal reparation and condemnation for *war crimes*.

In cases where the genocidal actions of one of the parties in a conflict are justified by a war-centric perspective, this definition is primarily used to defend the ethical and political legitimacy of the decision to go to war. The use of both representations – first a civil war, then genocide – creates a supposed break in the legal continuity, allowing for legal intervention to be legitimized only from the moment the war became a campaign of extermination of the population. This establishes a temporal division between the two events.

Some people argue that the "revolutionary war" had an impact on the entire Argentine population, since the defeat of the revolution presumably led to a loss of rights and opportunities for the lower classes and a general setback in the class struggle. However, even if this were true, the impact or affected parties would have been indirect and would not be relevant for a legal discourse assigning responsibility or determining whether crimes were committed.

What is clear is that in the various versions of the first narrative model, the concepts of "victim" and "affected person" do not fit well with a discourse about war or revolution. In these types of historical events, there are no perpetrators, victims, affected persons or crimes, but rather a political struggle that takes on a military aspect. The resolution of this social conflict has consequences that the participants must take responsibility for.

2 On the other hand, for those who believe that a genocide took place, the "passive subject of the crime" is constructed as the Argentine national group. It is not individual citizens or specific subjects who are primarily affected, but rather the group as a whole. This is why the term "genocide" is used, as it refers to the attempt to completely or partially destroy a group. By focusing on the intention to harm the group, a different concept of affected parties is proposed. Even the perpetrators are affected in a sense. Their transformation into torturers or murderers leaves a lasting impact on them and on the group as a whole. It causes severe damage to social bonds, different from that caused by any other conflict, including war. The notion of society as the "affected party" will lead to significant differences

in other areas of analysis, and this is why survivors and some human rights organizations have argued for the need to bring the dispute over the use of the term genocide before the justice system.

3 A binary division reappears in the discourse of the "terrorist state" or "crimes against humanity." However, there is no confrontation between more or less symmetrical sides, as in the discourse of war or that of the two demons. Instead, the strictly liberal duality between the state and the individual citizen's rights is emphasized. Through its punitive practices, the state allegedly violated the rights of many of the individuals it was supposed to protect and guarantee. Therefore, the passive subjects of the crime or those who were "affected" are the citizens whose rights were violated by the covert and illegal actions of the repressive apparatus.

Of course, some would accept that these citizens stand for *all* citizens, insofar as there were different ways of suffering state terror. The great difference, however, lies in the fact that from this perspective that they were affected "as citizens," whereas from the perspective of genocide they were affected "as a group."

Theoretical discussions about *totalitarianism* are based on liberal approaches, expressed in concepts such as crimes against humanity that focus on the conflict of authority between "state repression" and "individual autonomy." This conflict is at the heart of the democratic critique of state terror processes, as they involve the violation of human rights, which are basic rights of each individual. This is why "crimes against humanity" have no statute of limitations: they are seen as violating the basic human rights of every member of the population.

However, despite challenges to the dominant discourse of the "two demons," liberal interpretations of "state terrorism" are gradually becoming more widespread in legal and academic circles, replacing the previous dominant narrative with a model that ultimately maintains a similar logic. This shift is happening despite the ongoing resistance of many human rights organizations to this "liberal democratic" understanding of the impacts of state crimes, including organizations that support the concept of crimes against humanity. However, understanding events as crimes against humanity or state terrorism has an inherent contradiction: those who argue the need to fight the revolutionary challenge to citizens' rights then challenge the same liberal rights themselves. Ironically, this contradiction is often pointed out by the perpetrators in their own defense.

Zygmunt Bauman has studied how failed projects to transform society have given rise to a shift in the utopian horizon from the pursuit of social justice to a demand for the basic guarantees of citizenship, such as life and physical integrity (2001). It is also worth noting the connection between this way of thinking and the subsequent way in which "crimes against humanity" have been used to legitimize neo-colonial military interventions under the pretext of "responsibility to protect." The most prominent example was the bombing of the Libyan people in 2011 and the military intervention to overthrow the Khaddaffi's dictatorial regime. This was done to install a government more aligned with U.S. and European interests, particularly in terms of managing Libyan oil and controlling a strategically important region (Feierstein, 2019).

One more question regarding identity: National group or political group?

There has been some debate in Argentina about the identity of the people affected by the events in question. This has occurred both within the narrative of genocide and between those who believe the events were a genocide and those who believe they were acts of terrorism or crimes against humanity.

The exclusion of political groups from the final draft of the Convention on Genocide and its consequences has been extensively addressed in other works. However, this issue helps to understand why some of those who advocate for the concept of "political group" do not accept the legal definition of genocide, while others do accept the concept of genocide and also understand those affected as a "political group."

This section aims to examine the implications of these different perspectives for the way we remember and understand the events in question. It is important to note that the legal classification of the victims as one or the other is not the main focus of this analysis, rather the focus is on the effects these different classifications have on the processes of memory.

Many people who argue that it is necessary to define "those affected" as a political group do so because they believe that using the category of "national group" would "depoliticize" the victims, which would make it difficult to understand that the killing was motivated by political goals. They argue that using this category would obscure the political nature of the events in question (Crenzel, 2011).

This focus on politics, however, would seem simplistic, even overly so. Even though the concept of "political group" is present, the way in which it is defined as "partisan" and contrasted with wider society paradoxically depoliticizes it. The result is that the political group is excluded from the concept of "national group" and, therefore, from the category of genocide. In short, the attempt to politicize the victims can actually result in its opposite.

The concept of genocide as "partial destruction of a national group" was created as a way to address the exclusion of certain political groups from the Genocide Convention. However, this concept has had unexpected and significant impacts on how genocide is understood and how people are able to cope with it. As often happens, such decisions have unintended consequences for the processes of memory.

One of the most significant aspects of this new representation of genocide is that it allows us to understand the role of massive state violence in shaping and transforming identity. By framing the experience as the "destruction of the Argentine national group," we can see how the entire national population, as a collective, was affected by the violence and terror inflicted upon them. This narrative model has great power because it suggests that what was targeted for destruction was *our own group*, which can make the absence of the other feel like a loss of a part of oneself. This can help to bridge the gap between direct victims and society at large and alleviate feelings of alienation.

If we recognize that identity, especially collective identity, is constantly evolving, then the destruction of certain social relationships and identities (such as national, ethnic, political, religious, sexual, etc.) can have a profound impact on the identity of the whole group. By eliminating certain elements of identity, we are effectively amputating a part of ourselves that could have been a potential part of our own identity. The otherness of the victim (the "direct victim") is transformed in this way, and can be appropriated by a much broader segment of the population. At the same time, we are able to see the way in which groups have been stigmatized in order to marginalize them.

This shift in perspective, from empathy toward victims to identification with them as part of one's own identity, allows us to question and challenge our collective identities when faced with the consequences of terror. Rather than viewing the victims as "others" with whom we can feel empathy, we recognize that the terror affects our own identity as a group. It allows us to reconceptualize terror as something that impacts us, and not just others. This can be seen as a way to move beyond the typical liberal discourse that focuses on empathy for the victims, and instead to consider the wider implications of massive state violence for our own identities and collective experiences.

The use of the term "national group" in defining genocide, then, has a much more profound and powerful political impact than simply characterizing the victims as belonging to "political groups." This is because the idea of a "national group" allows us to understand the effects of terror on our own collective identity, rather than seeing the victims as "others" who are separate from us. When we view the victims as "others" – that is, alien to our collective identity –, it becomes more difficult to cope with the effects of terror and to work through them. This is because the process of healing can only work when we are able to engage with our own identity, rather than the identity of others.

We will also see the significant differences between these two conceptualizations in constructing a legacy for future generations. This process of passing on experiences from one generation (those who lived through the events) to the next will be explored further in section f).

Meaning or "causality"

The narratives of war, genocide and state terrorism also assign different meanings to massive state crimes. When considered as war, the predominant meaning of a conflict is often analyzed through the lens of "defeat" or "victory." From a military perspective, different ideological viewpoints generally agree that the Argentine military regime achieved a clear victory. For some perpetrators, victory was total and justified the restoration of democracy. Argentina's last *de facto* president, Reynaldo Benito Bignone, justified the "excesses" committed on the basis of "the democracy that we have bequeathed to the Argentine people" (Bignone, 2000). Others, however, noted that military victory was not accompanied by victory in the cultural sphere. They believed that this would inevitably lead to the regrouping of the enemy forces and their return to political action.[12] Thus, victory was incomplete as the state did not succeed in destroying the socio-cultural roots of the opposition. This may be due to the military abandoning power earlier than planned after the disastrous Falklands-Malvinas War against Great Britain in 1982.

For those in the opposing ideological-political camp, who view the conflict as a "civil war" or "revolutionary war," the focus is on interpreting and understanding the "military defeat" in order to slowly rebuild the popular forces and learn from the lessons of terror and extermination. This process is seen as a necessary step toward eventually escalating the conflict again under more favorable conditions.

In both of these perspectives, we see what could be called a "defensive causality," in which the repressive violence is seen as a response to a previous disruption caused by insurgent action, and its ultimate goal is to maintain the status quo and prevent change. From the perspective of genocide, however, the meaning of the process goes beyond the simple binary logic of war. If the goal was to fundamentally reorganize social relationships, then what is most significant is the irreversible nature of these social and historical processes (even if the same could also be said about the effects of war).[13]

While in a defeat the focus is on analyzing the details of the fighting and the conditions under which it occurred, in a genocide the emphasis is on understanding how social relationships and the affected group itself (in this case, the Argentine national group) have been transformed. The objective of a genocide is not necessarily to achieve a victory over a specific military or social force, but rather to fundamentally and qualitatively transform the functioning of society as a whole. In other words, the goal of a genocide is not to simply defeat a particular enemy, but rather to fundamentally alter the fabric of society.

When analyzing the impact of a genocide, it can be very useful to consider the notion of liberation from microdespotisms in various social structures such as the family, school, work or prisons (O'Donnell, 1997). This approach can help us to understand the economic and social transformations that occurred in Argentina as a result of the terror, and how these changes affected the functioning of society (Aspiazu et al., 2003). The most important aspect of this analysis is to understand how social functioning was transformed by the terror, both during and after the dictatorship. By focusing on the "destruction of the group" rather than the "destruction of individuals," we can more fully grasp the ways in which the terror impacted society as a whole and how it has been internalized even after it no longer operates openly.

In this narrative of genocide, the purpose of repression is no longer "defensive," but rather "offensive." Violence is not just a response to insurgent action, nor is it simply intended to maintain the status quo. Instead, it seeks to fundamentally alter the status quo in a negative sense, and the presence of insurgent groups is used as an excuse for transformations that are achieved through terror. In other words, terror is not simply a means of defending against a perceived threat; it is a means of actively and intentionally transforming society in a negative way.

It is noteworthy that numerous military documents from the late 1960s show repression was intended to bring about social change. At the time, this was a partly a response to the Peronist resistance led by the exiled Peron himself and partly to the appearance of the first Cuban-inspired guerrillas, the so-called Uturuncos at the end of 1959. The army made short work of the Uturuncos and similar tiny and incipient organizations in military courts but the Peronist resistance (more political than military) proved more difficult to control, hence the development of a plan to control society by more radical means.

Finally, the vision of "state terrorism" often revolves around the opposition between state and individual, particularly with regards to the protection of individual freedoms and rights. This perspective is linked to the idea that the state can destroy the rights of the persons through its oppressive machinery. As a result, individuals become subservient and unable to fully exercise their freedoms. Oppression can be motivated by either defensive or offensive reasons, but it is primarily characterized by the state's increasing ability to punish persons and infringe on their rights. It should be noted that this vision does not take into account the historical context in which social bonds are formed and broken, but rather focuses on the state's power to punish individuals.

The question of analogies (the use of the past in the present)

Another aspect to consider in the relationship between memory and the present is the way in which different narrative models connect with events from the past. This connection can have significant consequences for how we understand and use representations of the past to inform our actions, learning, and decisions for the present and future. It is important to consider the specific events that are being referenced and how they are being interpreted and utilized in order to understand the full impact of these narrative models on our understanding of the past and its relevance to the present.

Narratives about civil or revolutionary wars often connect past events to experiences of revolution in countries such as Russia, Cuba, Nicaragua and El Salvador. However, these narratives may overlook the devastating nature of such wars and the systematic destruction that can occur as a result. For example, the Argentine experience included significant levels of destruction, but this aspect may be downplayed or ignored in narratives about other revolutionary processes in Latin America, such as the Cuban revolution. In some cases, such as El Salvador and possibly Guatemala, the phenomena of revolutionary and counter-revolutionary war and genocide are interconnected; but if one aspect is prioritized, the other may be minimized or dismissed, thus reducing genocide to a by-product of the revolutionary struggle. This can have significant consequences for memory processes, as it may prevent a full understanding of the specific nature of genocide as deliberate destruction.

Representations of genocide often take the Nazis as a paradigmatic case, even though there have been numerous instances of mass extermination in other historical contexts. While analogies with the Nazis are useful, they can also have some drawbacks. For example, the racist ideology of Nazism had little to do with what happened in Latin America and Argentina. Indeed, describing the extermination of the indigenous population in Guatemala as racist obscures the political motives behind the genocide, a tendency also found in memories of Nazism. This can be problematic because it may prevent a full understanding of the specific characteristics and motivations behind a particular genocide.

However, the concept of "partial destruction of the national group" can help us move beyond framing exterminations as motivated solely by racism (as in Nazi-occupied Europe or in Guatemala). It allows for a more nuanced understanding, including the ways in which populations have been affected by massive state violence and the collective interpellation arising from this experience. It also highlights the diverse responsibilities and consequences linked to this extermination, and can help transform the narratives around memory and the ways in which memory is constructed and appropriated.

On the other hand, the analogy with Nazism can also have a positive impact on memory. Most significantly, it can lead to the recognition of massive state violence as a crime for which there can be no impunity. In Argentina, for example, popular rejection of impunity was expressed through the slogan "Like the Nazis, we will hunt them down wherever they go." While the trials of Nazi criminals may not have been as extensive or as just as they are portrayed in collective memory, the idea that these crimes are imprescriptible and that impunity is unacceptable has persisted in Argentina and has been fueled in part by the use of the term genocide and the analogy with Nazism. This has been the case despite efforts by legal experts to oppose any comparison along these lines.

Narratives about the "terrorist state" or crimes against humanity are not necessarily focused on the past, but rather on the future. These narratives are often linked to numerous human rights violations in the past, but their primary purpose is to create new and more comprehensive international institutions (such as the International Tribunals, the International Criminal Court and international and inter-American Human Rights Conventions) to address such crimes. In many cases, these regulations and institutions were created after the Argentine military dictatorship. These narratives therefore serve to shape the future by promoting mechanisms to prevent and address crimes against humanity and state terrorism.

Appeals to human rights to justify criminal law interventions, as seen in the 2011 invasion of Libya, can complicate the analogy between past and present cases of crimes against humanity. This could allow Argentina's recent traumas to be used as a justification for international intervention under the "responsibility to protect" civilian populations (Feierstein, 2009, 2019). Paradoxically, this could serve as a new tool for legitimizing neo-imperial conquest in the 21st century, at a time when support for the anticommunist crusade and the "war on terror" is fading. The main thing is to consider the ways in which the past is invoked and the motivations for doing so in order to fully understand the implications of such analogies and their potential consequences.

It is highly significant that the concept of crimes against humanity has been chosen to apply criminal law in the context of international interventions. This concept is relatively lax and ambiguous compared to other concepts in international criminal law, such as war crimes and genocide, which have more specific and restrictive definitions. This makes it easier to justify interventions under the "responsibility to protect" civilian populations, as any media denunciation can potentially be used to justify such action. However, it also means that any act of state violence, and even some non-state acts of violence, can be classified as crimes against humanity, regardless of whether there is clear territorial control or intent to destroy a group, as is required for war crimes or genocide, respectively. This vagueness in defining crimes against humanity can make it easier to invoke this concept to justify interventions, but it can also lead to a broad application of the concept that may not accurately reflect the specific circumstances of each case.

As a result, analogies between different instances of crimes against humanity can lead to confounding very different events. This can be seen in the way catchwords such as "the century of genocides," serve to legitimize and morally justify actions where violence is not necessarily systematic or state-sponsored. Paradoxically, interventions designed to "prevent" crimes against humanity can end up doing more harm than good. The tools that were created to hold perpetrators accountable are then used to justify the actions of the intervening powers. It is important to carefully consider the specific context and motivations of each case in order to address the issue of crimes against humanity properly.

Consequences

The meaning and consequences of an experience such as war are constructed through the process of linking the present with the past and drawing analogies. If the aim of war is to defeat the enemy totally or partially, the result will be a shift in the balance of power. Independently of ideology, those who believe there was a war in Argentina tend to agree that the revolution was crushed or, at the very least, postponed for a very long term. According to those who supported the regime, subversion was completely eradicated or at least completely disarmed and confined to the political and cultural sphere. For those who opposed the regime, the balance of power tilted toward the regime, and explains certain economic policies at the expense of the poorer sectors of the population.

If terror aimed to reshape the social fabric, its consequences were not only to be found in the advance of capitalism and the loss of rights among the poorer sectors of society. It also brought a profound transformation of social life, from the family to employment, from politics to religion. These macro-political and, especially, micro-political transformations distinguish the consequences of war from those of genocide. The fact that the primary focus was not armed combat, casualties, or territory, but rather the concentration camp, meant that terror radiated outwards from the bodies of those broken by the concentration camp system to those who sensed its silent, distressing, and sinister effects. This is the meaning of the "mark," where *that which could not be* affects all the subsequent events, which can only be understood in relation to this absence (Feierstein, 2012, 2015b).

The subsequent apolitical, indifferent and individualistic attitudes of the following years in Argentina cannot be explained by the unfavorable balance of political and military forces alone. The genocidal regime brought about a deep and significant transformation of the social bond itself, which may have even affected the possibilities of transmitting experiences across generations. This is, of course, linked to the global balance of power and the end of the Cold War.

This breakdown of the social bond operates in various ways, but one of the most devastating is the reification by the left of the generation that lived through the terror as the "first and only," a process that turns subsequent generations into "orphans" in every sense. This can happen for two reasons: Either they are made to bear the burden of deaths they neither fully own nor fully understand, or they are confronted with a generation unable to transmit its own experience coherently. This generation oscillates between idealizing its murdered "heroes" and renouncing the utopias it once defended. These are not only mutually contradictory positions; both close off the possibility of generating a transgenerational legacy and a *chain of transmission*.

Finally, according to the perspective of "state terrorism," the consequences were not so negative as in the other two narratives, precisely because of the reinterpretation implicit in the fundamental "dictatorship-democracy" divide. The moral collapse of the dictatorship and the delegitimizing of the military, from this perspective, led to a rejection of dictatorial regimes in general. This notion became firmly established during the 1980s and has continued throughout the post-dictatorship period. It has also led to a new and valuable concern for human rights and respect for individual guarantees. Thus, despite the horrors of the dictatorship, the return to democracy is seen as definitive, and the negative consequences are linked to the still-present marks of repressive policing – overcrowded prison conditions, "trigger-happy" police, criminal networks linked to the police structure, networks of corruption, etc. For, it is argued, totalitarian states were delegitimized by the widespread and systematic human rights violations committed during the last dictatorship.

It is interesting that the human rights organizations most closely linked to this type of discourse have focused on denouncing the still-present marks of authoritarian rule, while others continue to be more concerned with the social and economic consequences of terror in the present. The two approaches do not necessarily contradict one another, although they clearly show the effects of representing the past in different ways.

One of the most enduring conclusions of these state terrorism narratives is the need to collectively reject previous violence and to uphold unlimited respect for citizens' rights. Violence must be denounced, whether revolutionary or repressive, during times of war or social change. This is seen as a costly but fundamental learning consequence following the exercise of illegal and clandestine state punitive power that characterized the 1970s.

Now, there is no doubt that such learning is important, but we need to know to what extent it helps or hinders working through the consequences of terror. This will be discussed in greater depth in the final section.

Healing and prevention

Different accounts of the causes and consequences of massive state crimes – including who it affects and how – do not only lead to different historical analogies. Each perspective suggests the need for different actions *in the present*, and it is at this point that representations take on their most political meaning, as well as their ultimate purpose: linking memory with action.

For those who support the idea of a "dirty war against subversion," what lies ahead is "rearmament" in the "cultural struggle." Trials have begun again and the perpetrators remain delegitimized in the eyes of the public. Consequently, there is a need to stop considering the "so-called victims" as "angels" and reformulate our understanding of the years prior to the dictatorship from this position. Perhaps the most successful and prolific exponent of this position has been Juan Bautista Yofre. Yofre highlights the violence of the guerrilla movements and equates it with state violence, generalizing responsibilities as a way of creating a "shared complicity" in exercising terror.[14]

For those who hold the opposite view within the war discourse (that is, that there was a counter-revolutionary war that ended in the defeat of the popular sectors), the present moment would imply the need for "rearmament." Now would be the time to regroup the surviving forces, and – taking the changes in structural and economic-political conditions more or less into account – to propose when a new offensive could begin.

In truth, this idea is no longer widely held by any political, intellectual, or academic group in Argentina. But it is difficult to imagine any other coherent way of linking the past with the present with this narrative of counter-revolutionary war. The only action it proposes – in an increasingly abstract way – is the need to process the effects of defeat. This proposal gradually loses its meaning as the years go by, when the generations in question are increasingly less able to identify or even connect with the so-called war.

It is also important to point out that no organization in Argentina today advocates a return to revolutionary armed struggle. Indeed, insurgent violence is completely absent from the contemporary Argentine political agenda. Therefore, it is surprising to hear journalists, politicians and academics constantly urging surviving actors to abjure political violence and carry out collective repentance.

For those who support the notion of genocide, the ways of working through the past are quite different. The whole of the national group has been affected. Thus, the healing process needs to be collective. The social transformations brought about cannot be changed by mere acts of will, for they are necessarily rooted in the unconscious, as pointed out in Chapters 1 and 2. Any attempt at reform must take into account the tremendous force of what Freud called repetition compulsion, the mind's need to reproduce unprocessed trauma over and over again. To this we must add pacts of denial, a social phenomenon that helps to keep individual trauma repressed, as well as the various processes of *desensitization* that accompany such pacts.

From this perspective, mindlessly repeating the slogan "never again" can also be an act of denial. For if the phrase is used to mean: "Let's put the trauma or the catastrophe behind us," it will not work. Only a profound analysis of the complex marks left by trauma on the unconscious mind and symbolically in collective representations can contribute to the slow and patient work of healing.

As survivors and their contemporaries engage in heated debates about whether the events should be labeled as genocide, we may be unknowingly moving toward something more complex. Many human rights organizations, political groups, children and relatives of the disappeared, state institutions and health groups are actively participating in discussions contributing to a collective, *eminently political* process of working through the trauma. Even some courts, judges and prosecutors are doing the same.

With perspectives of "state terrorism" or "crimes against humanity," the healing process tends to face many obstacles. It is within this perspective that we see the most denial – people who try to sweep the past under the rug and lump all violence together (subversive action and state repression). In these perspectives, the balance of power (an important theme in discussions on war) and the process of healing and understanding the changes in society and social connections (key themes in discussions about genocide) do not really come into play. Instead, justice is seen as a way to put the past behind us and move on from a problematic relationship between political groups – some people would say within society in general – and "violence."

This is a focus on working through "violence" (i.e., managing aggression in the abstract) rather than on the social reorganization produced by state repression. As such, it is to be found in the work of Hugo Vezzetti (2002) or Marcos Novaro and Vicente Palermo (2003).

Views such as these that try to lump together different instances of violence and simplify them end up reinstating binary thinking in a more subtle and powerful way than the theory of the two demons itself. Once again, they equate the responsibility of those who provoked the horror with that of those who carried it out. Even if some of them try to differentiate between one use of violence and another, the "action-reaction" model still perpetuates denial. This way, the fact that the social changes brought about by terror were relatively independent and separate from how much different political or cultural groups supported insurgent violence is ignored, and so the levels of responsibility for each action get mixed up. The insurgents are held responsible for a plan to change society using terror that went beyond what the armed left-wing groups could actually do, since this was not their main goal.

Calling state actions "terrorist" suggests an indiscriminate use of violence, which is what terrorism means. In other words, these actions are not targeted and they affect everyone. When this is combined with calling all insurgent actions in Argentina "terrorist" (a label that has no any real definition of terrorism attached to it, unlike Basque, Irish, Algerian or Palestinian insurgent groups, who did use terrorist tactics), we are back again with the idea of two sides with similar approaches, which was at the core of both war stories and the so-called "theory of the two demons."

The binary model of understanding the experience of terror persists, but it would be incorrect to attribute this persistence to a conspiracy. Instead, this model is effective for the psychic construction of the generation who lived through the repressive period, particularly for those who were not directly involved as perpetrators or victims. The denialist character of this model leads to its constant reappearance (Feierstein, 2012).

As I have repeatedly pointed out in this book, our minds constantly seek to understand and make sense of our experiences, especially those that have left a traumatic impact. Demonizing violence in any form allows us to deny the ways in which social practices have been transformed by terror and block the possibility of their return, thus alienating us from our past. Instead, we have a meaningless condemnation of violence in the abstract, an equalizing of responsibilities, and a redefinition of justice and equality as "recognition of" or "respect for individual rights." All these processes may act together to create what has already been referred to as "ideologies of meaninglessness."[15]

Effects on generational transmission, on the possibility of mourning and on form of appropriation and alienation

If the model of state terrorism is the most effective way to understand the denial of meaning in contemporary events, it is worthwhile to consider the potential consequences of different ways of coping with grief and how these representations may be passed down to future generations. Abraham and Torok have proposed the concept of a "pantheon" or "crypt" to examine this issue:

> When the possibility of incorporating a loss is not present, the only option may be to deny the loss completely and act as if it never happened. This means not sharing grief with others and internalizing all unspoken words, unexpressed emotions, and unshed tears along with the trauma of the loss. This process of unspoken mourning creates a secret pantheon within the individual.
>
> *(Abraham & Torok, 2005, p. 38)*

Abraham and Torok suggest that the pantheon or crypt exists as long as there is a "mutilated self." They argue that the common goal in these situations is to conceal the wound because it is unspeakable and the mere act of speaking about it would be destructive. The specific circumstances may vary, but the underlying desire to hide the wound remains the same. Different coping mechanisms may be used to obscure the wound and prevent it being revealed (Abraham & Torok, 2005, p. 266).

According to the Centro de Salud Mental y Derechos Humanos de Chile (CINTRAS), these repressed experiences that are not fully processed in one generation are unconsciously passed down to the next generation. This can have a lasting impact on how grief is understood and dealt with in future generations:

> The contents of the pantheon or crypt are unspeakable for the individual because, although they are present in the person's psyche, the person cannot verbalize them. When transmitted to the next generation, these unprocessed experiences take the form of a "ghost" that cannot be represented in words. This makes them unmentionable, and the contents are ignored, but their existence can still cause mental disturbances. In future generations, these repressed experiences may manifest as bizarre symptoms, sensations, and emotions that seem unrelated to the family's psychological life, as they are unaware of the hidden trauma that has not been resolved.
> *(CINTRAS, 2009, pp. 48–49)*

Haydeé Faimberg has referred to the transgenerational transmission of trauma as "generational telescoping" or "alienating identification," as the experiences of one generation become embedded in the life history of their children and/or grandchildren (Faimberg, 1996). This phenomenon can be seen in the way that the narratives being analyzed contribute to the transgenerational transmission of memory.

The generational impact of war and state terrorism can lead to a legacy of relative incoherence in their respective discourses. In the case of war, this is due to the transformation of the conflict's narrative into a heroic depiction of the absent, which is often accompanied by a melancholic mode of mourning. In the case of state terrorism, the denialist nature of the discourse leads to a generalized condemnation of an abstract and equalized violence, resulting in a detached attitude toward the events.[16]

However, in Argentina, since the end of the Cold War, there has not been a militarized view of social conflict, and the centralized repressive state has been delegitimized. Therefore, both the perspectives of war and state terrorism present views of the past that are difficult to understand and appropriate for a generation that has not experienced war. This generation, despite the issues and problems faced by contemporary Argentine democracy, has lived for several decades in a regime that has been legitimized by the majority of the population, and where the limits to freedom of expression do not come from the state, but rather from media corporations or certain economic groups.

This being so, the generation of those born after the dictatorship may feel a certain disconnection from these two discourses. The attempt to link those who did not experience these events (the majority of the Argentine population today) to these discourses can feel "forced," as neither the war nor the "democracy-dictatorship" dichotomy poses a present or future threat. This has been the case since the early 1990s, when the last military uprising led by Mohamed Alí Seineldín was suppressed, resulting in the death of 15 coup leaders, the imprisonment of numerous rebels and the more or less permanent subordination of the Armed Forces to civilian power.

Therefore, the criticism and self-criticism of the widespread use of violence in Argentina before and during the dictatorship may not address the everyday reality (nearly 40 years later) of a generation born after the dictatorship. These two interpretations of war and state terrorism tend to create an increasingly "alienated" perspective in the second generation, relegating the events of terror to just another chapter in history, a history that belongs to their parents but is not necessarily connected to their own present-day experiences.

The earlier generation's inability to pass on a legacy to its children has a number of complex and profound effects. The younger generation has responded with behaviors such as the "escraches" organized by HIJOS – public demonstrations outside the perpetrators' homes or places they frequent. "Identity Theatre," and the work of poets such as Juan Terranova are similarly products of a generation born during or just before the military coup. So, too, are films such as Albertina Carri's *Los rubios*, and the complete film work of Alejandro Agresti.

In 2011, Elsa Drucaroff published a book that explored the challenges of transmitting the generational legacy in post-dictatorship literary works (Drucaroff, 2011). Drucaroff, who has written extensively on this topic, describes the two ways in which this legacy is hindered and delegitimized. Firstly, there is the heroic register: This denies successive generations any possibility of innovation. Secondly, there is denial. This prevents any legacy being transmitted at all. The book compares the biases of the generation that lived through the genocide with the actual work produced by writers born after 1960.

It is worth noting, however, that Drucaroff's book makes the same mistake for which she criticizes literary critics such as David Viñas and Beatriz Sarlo. Drucaroff claims they are unable to see anything new in post-dictatorship writers because they are convinced the avant-garde ended with them and their persecution. She says these critics are not even interested in reading their work of the younger generation. And yet Drucaroff falls into the same trap when discussing the essayists and historians of the generation she seeks to defend:

> The scarcity of essayists, that is, of writers who dare to publish and defend their own original thinking about Argentine society, its culture, its history, its politics, its past and its present, is striking. It is not that they do not have their own thoughts; these are conveyed in the fiction they produce. But it is as if they only allow themselves to express them through the alibi

of fiction, through the dreamlike and unconscious resources with which art expresses its political contestation of the established order.

(Drucaroff, 2011, p. 188)

This is a clear example of the unconscious power of denialist mechanisms in the generation of those who lived through the genocide. As an essayist, Drucaroff tries to dismantle them, but only succeeds in doing so in the specific realm of literature. She is unable to recognize the contradiction or absurdity of characterizing this generation as capable of contestation in one field but not in others. Like Viñas with imaginative literature, Drucaroff seems to have little interest in acknowledging the work of essayists, historians or social scientists.

Obviously, analyzing the effects of the three narrative models on the discursivity of *another* generation requires a more comprehensive and complex understanding of the various impacts and spheres in the processes of memory and representation, as well as their connections to action.

The "escrache" signaled the irruption of the second generation (the children of those who lived through the dictatorship) into the silence passively accepted out of fear or in the name of "reconciliation." As mentioned earlier, this consisted of publicly harassing and shaming the perpetrators, often outside their homes. It took place specifically between 1990 and 2005, when there was complete impunity and the buzzword was "reconciliation."

"Escraches" are a political, not a literary practice and one that is performed intentionally, not subconsciously. They were not just a milestone in the fight against impunity, but part of a wider range of efforts including bringing cases to courts in other countries, pursuing "truth trials," opening cases for crimes exempt from impunity laws, attempting to nullify those laws, and holding regular public demonstrations on March 24th (commemoration of the coup d´etat) and December 10th (commemoration of the end of the dictatorship). These actions were all part of the ongoing struggle against impunity, which should not overlook the efforts of those who were involved at the time of the events.

However, the "escraches" represented a generational challenge – a refusal to allow the transmission of the traumatic legacy to be interrupted. They were a cry of rebellion that sought and continues to seek a connection not only with the disappeared parents, but also with a generation that has failed to fulfill its parental responsibilities, including its role in exercising justice and authority as "law givers." The "escraches" were a way for this generation to demand that their parents' absence be acknowledged and that justice be served.

The "escrache" challenged the State to take responsibility for the crimes committed during the dictatorship. The failure of those who lived through the genocide to take responsibility has led to a rebellion against a law and order, on the grounds that a society that denies justice is inviable. This challenge is directed at the State, but it also speaks to a whole generation, highlighting their failure to fulfill their paternal roles. It rejects their authority because it lacks justice.

This challenge can also be seen in the literary, artistic and creative works of the second generation. Some question, others confront. Some are by the children of the disappeared, others by children of those who experienced organized terror. These works reflect the ongoing struggle for justice and the interpellation of those who have failed to take responsibility for the atrocities of the past.

Juan Terranova's work (2004) challenges an entire generation to take responsibility for the past. One could say that this is a "generational battle cry" that is deeply disturbing for many, including the children of that generation and the writer himself. This "battle cry" highlights the disruption in the transmission of the traumatic legacy and accuses a whole generation of collectively positioning themselves as victims (within the "state terrorism" perspective) while also being perpetrators. This allows them to deny responsibility by assigning it to military and insurgent groups. They claim the right to receive reparations (economic, political, symbolic) while avoiding any responsibility in the present to their peers, let alone to future generations.

A *refusal to accept responsibility* is not made up for by simply condemning violence in abstract terms, without taking concrete action in the present. This might include economic sacrifices and actively taking responsibility for the limitations and failures of the past, as well as generously passing on the values received from one's own parents, a legacy that the genocide generation has never acknowledged.

Embarking on a journey involving a generational transmission of legacy means sacrificing one's time and wishes – perhaps even one's social position – to make way for future generations. Instead, most people tend to present themselves as eternal rebels rather than acknowledging their debt to their ancestors. Combined with the traumatic effects of terror, this hinders the possibility of passing on a painful but necessary legacy. Instead, the self-criticism of violence seems to be used as a way to maintain their role as vanguard, avoiding both the legacy of their predecessors and the possibility of facing criticism from their successors.

"El ignorante," one of the most controversial and disputed poems by Terranova, accuses the generation of contemporaries of being "parricides and filicides" because their "only real and successful operation was to survive." This is a harsh criticism that highlights the irreverent anger of the poet toward the way in which the hegemonic discourses of his contemporaries have condemned their children to *a non-place, a position of being in the place of an absent other who can never be fully incorporated or mourned.*

This critical view suggests that the generation of contemporaries has failed to take responsibility for their actions and has instead prioritized their own survival.

Leaving aside its irreverence and its author's later positions, "El ignorante" also highlights how the genocide generation have refused to transmit their experiences and knowledge to both past and future generations. As a result of their traumatic experiences, they have become detached from the conditions that gave rise to their revolutionary project and have denied any possibility of it being appropriated by future generations. Whether they view their project as heroic or completely reject it, they have denied any meaningful role or place to their successors. In both cases, the successors are excluded from this history. Either the second generation end up concluding that they will never be so heroic as the first or they are unable to learn from the first generation's self-criticism that denies any utopian purpose. This denial of a legacy and a place for future generations has significant ethical consequences and reflects the ways in which the generation of contemporaries has failed to take responsibility for their actions and the impact they have had on society.

Albertina Carri's film *Los rubios* also challenges the meaning constructed by the generation of contemporaries, particularly the way it idealizes the disappeared. In their attempts to offer a posthumous symbolic justice to the disappeared, the contemporaries leave no possible place for their children other than that of a failed or depleted copy. Carri's film rejects this role, as it does not allow her an opportunity to create something new; she can only be an impoverished reproduction of the past. *Los rubios*, then, reflects the ways in which the generation of contemporaries has denied the possibility of meaningful transmission or incorporation for their successors and has instead imposed a narrow and limiting role on them.

Gabriel Gatti, who is the son of a disappeared person and has analyzed the phenomenon of disappearance in depth, tries to address these issues by stating that "meaning is where the battle is fought" (Gatti, 2008, p. 46). He argues that the problem for the children of the disappeared is how to speak "from the void," a void in which a generation that finds no meaning in the narratives produced by the contemporaries of the catastrophe may feel lost. Gatti distinguishes between a "narrative of meaning" (typical of the contemporaries) and a "narrative of the absence of meaning" (typical of their children). This distinction is useful, and we have already encountered something similar in Drucaroff. Nevertheless, Gatti's use of the term "narrative of the absence of meaning" may be problematic, as it suggests that the children of the disappeared are striving to "take control of a life that develops within an impossible" and to "inhabit an already institutionalized absence" (Gatti, 2008, p. 25). While Gatti accurately identifies the difficulties that the successor generation faces in constructing meaning, he suggests that these problems can be resolved through "management" of or "coexistence" with this absence.[17]

It may be useful to consider Gatti's view from a different, more methodological perspective, one that takes into account the whole of this current volume. From this perspective, it is worth questioning why some narratives produced by contemporaries are considered "meaningful" while others, viewed from the perspective of the children of the disappeared, are seen as an "absence of meaning." Instead of an "absence of meaning," what is evident in the approaches of Terranova, Agresti, Carri and others of their generation (including Gatti himself) is the inability to appropriate or reproduce the meanings of the previous generation. This has effectively closed off the possibility of processing the catastrophe for both generations.[18]

Gatti's analysis of some of the responses to the catastrophe is original and insightful. Nevertheless, it could be further enriched by considering these works as an attempt, however messy or unsuccessful, to construct a *different* meaning rather than simply negotiating the *absence* of meaning. As we have seen, it is the questioning and search for meaning, rather than its absence, that enables us to process traumatic experiences. It is valuable, then, to observe the generational confrontations around the diverse and complex ways in which meaning is given to traumatic experiences, as this is a necessary step in working through them.

These discussions can be seen within a perspective that focuses on the social reorganization caused by state mass killing and the work of processing the trauma in both generations. The questions posed by the children of the disappeared challenge the denial prevalent among their parents and make it possible to transmit a legacy. By working together to construct a different meaning, both generations can confront the "crypt" and try to open its sealed lid together, seeking to understand and make sense of the traumatic experiences of the past. This process of joint meaning-making can help to promote a more inclusive and mutually supportive social bond, one that recognizes the intergenerational impacts of traumatic events and works toward a more equitable and just society.

The question of how social practices are shaped and reorganized by genocide is one that challenges both generations, although in different ways. To address this issue, it is necessary to engage in an intergenerational dialogue that openly confronts the pain, shame and guilt that have been inherited from the past. Through this dialogue, it may be possible to construct a legacy that includes the dreams, successes, problems and doubts of a generation that was affected by terror and its consequences while also striving for a better world.

Terror sought to destroy the existing meaning of life, reducing lived experience to meaninglessness, and block the possibility of protest. It aimed to reorganize the ways in which individuals understand themselves and their relationships with others, including their loved ones and even their own children.

One of the key findings of this first volume is that a primary goal of genocidal reorganization is to achieve *desubjectivation* and *desensitization* not only in the direct victims, but also in the social group targeted by the practices: the national group and its network of social relationships. When considering the ways in which violence is named and described, it is important to consider the relationship between the traumas experienced and the events being discussed. If definitions are adjusted without taking these connections into account, it may be difficult to fully understand what is being discussed and the effects it has on ourselves, our parents and our children. It is essential to consider the transfer relations between traumas and events in order to more fully comprehend the impact and significance of these experiences.

Different concepts and approaches may open different doors in this quest for understanding and responsibility. It is important that we are aware of these different approaches and are willing to consider them in order to better understand the experiences of the past and their ongoing impact on our lives and relationships. This requires a commitment to being attentive and responsible in our reflections and actions.

Notes

1 While it is possible to analyze the various descriptions and their underlying doctrine, this is a separate issue from the processes of memory and representation. The construction of judgments, on the other hand, will be addressed in more detail in the second volume of this work.
2 It will be seen below that Eduardo Luis Duhalde, who coined the term "terrorist state," linked it to the concept of genocide. However, the subsequent use of the term "state terrorism" has deviated significantly from the meaning that Duhalde originally intended.
3 This multiple categorization approach can be found in Inés Izaguirre et al (2009) and collaborators, *Lucha de clases, guerra civil y genocidio en la Argentina, 1973-1983. Antecedents. Development. Complicidades*, Buenos Aires, Eudeba, 2009, which explicitly juxtaposes the concepts of civil war and genocide, expressly excluding the category of crimes against humanity and less clearly that of state terrorism. Their book is based on the previous works of Juan Carlos Marín (1996), who begins by classifying events as war but quickly adopts the concept of genocide.
4 In contrast to its centrality in the experiences of countries like Spain and Uruguay, the concept of war has not been emphasized in discussions of Argentina's history. This lack of emphasis may be related to the legal actions taken in Argentina, which are based on the recognition of the state's unequal and asymmetrical power to punish certain groups. This understanding of the state's power challenges the traditional concept of war as a struggle between "equals."
5 It is important to recognize that the term "dirty war," which was coined and exclusively used by the perpetrators of human rights abuses in Argentina, has come to dominate foreign literature and international discussions about the country. In the 21st century, the term has started to appear in many Argentine academic

works without explaining its meaning or the ethical and political implications it carries as an inherited concept from French counterinsurgency doctrine. Examples of this usage can be found in Novaro and Palermo (2003).
6 The Argentine Human Rights Commission (CADHU) denounced the human rights abuses taking place in Argentina as early as March 1977, and referred to the events as a "process of genocide." From this point on, the genocidal nature of the events in Argentina and the use of the term "genocide" to describe them became more widely accepted. At the same time, there was growing doubt about the classification of the events as a war. Eduardo Luis Duhalde, a member of CADHU in exile, later served as Secretary of Human Rights during the governments of Néstor Kirchner and Cristina Fernández de Kirchner from 2003 to 2012.
7 Statements by the former de facto governor of the Province of Buenos Aires, Ibérico Saint Jean, to the *International Herald Tribune*, May 26, 1977.
8 International organizations have played a role in separating the horror of human rights abuses from the socioeconomic conditions that gave rise to them and influencing other human rights organizations in Latin America. For more information on this topic, see Naomi Klein (2010), especially Chapter 5 which discusses the role of the Ford Foundation in both promoting neoliberalism in conjunction with repressive regimes and in supporting certain approaches to "managing" horror through human rights organizations, museums and academic groups. This debate has also been taken up in Spanish and Argentine courts, where non-Argentine human rights organizations have made unusual and striking attempts to prevent the classification of the events in Argentina as genocide by different courts (national or international).
9 See, for example, the use of this concept in Hugo Vezzetti (2002) or in the work of Marcos Novaro and Vicente Palermo (2003), among numerous other works that focus on the consequences of the horror, while taking care not to delve into an analysis of the socioeconomic order that these horrors helped to create.
10 For a legal interpretation of the discourse surrounding the human rights abuses in Argentina, you may want to refer to the amicus curiae brief submitted by the Nizkor organization in the case brought in Spain against Adolfo Scilingo. The document, which can be found at www.radionizkor.org, was taken into consideration by the Spanish National Court in its decision to change the initial classification of the crimes from genocide to crimes against humanity.
11 For an extensive critique of this distinction, see Daniel Feierstein (2014), in particular Chapter 1.
12 See statements to the press and pleadings in the various trials of the perpetrators Massera, Camps, Harguindeguy, Menéndez and Bussi, among others, from 1985 to the present.
13 The concept of "irreversibility" in relation to social and historical processes does not mean that the consequences of these processes cannot be undone, as some postmodern theories might suggest, or that we must accept them with a cynical pragmatism. Rather, it means that social and historical events leave lasting impacts that make it impossible to return to the previous state as if they had never happened. These events are "irreversible" in the sense that we must address their effects and try to transform them, but we can no longer restore the conditions that existed before they occurred.
14 Joffre has been prolific, with one book per year and always in the same tone. All of them follow the same logic of avoiding responsibility, either through undifferentiated collective responsibility (*Fuimos todos* "We all did it," Yofre, 2007) or ignorance (*Nadie fue*: "Nobody did it," Yofre, 2006), approaches that seem contradictory but are in fact opposite sides of the same coin: levelling and equalizing responsibilities. For a contrary approach and of an incomparable theoretical level,

see the classic work by Karl Jaspers (1946), which should be mandatory material in Argentine schools and especially in journalism schools and on training courses for the armed security forces.
15 While this approach to understanding denial processes is based on a more nuanced and nonconspiratorial perspective, it is important to note that some individuals may have political motivations for denying certain events or ideas. These motivations could include a desire to legitimize certain businesses or economic systems that have arisen as a result of repression, or the use of human rights as a justification for neocolonial military intervention. It's also worth considering the role of organizations like the Ford Foundation, which has been involved in training "shock economists" and funding those who promote denialist views. However, the focus of this book is not on these specific political motivations, but rather on a deeper understanding of denial processes in general.
16 For an analysis of the different ways in which people experience and process grief, you may want to refer to Freud's classic work *Mourning and Melancholia* and the third and final volume of John Bowlby's trilogy *Attachment and Loss* (1973). In this volume, Bowlby provides a detailed analysis of the various forms of grief and their relationship to the potential development of detachment as a way of coping with the effects of absence.
17 It is suggestive that Gatti, despite being a "child of the disappeared," is generationally in the place that Susan Suleiman characterized as "generation 1.5" (Susan Rubin Suleiman, 2008), that is, those who were children during the course of the traumatic events, were not old enough to be contemporaries, but were somewhat older than most of their children, born during or after the events. Although Drucaroff (2011) characterizes these people as the first post-dictatorship generation, Suleiman's analysis is more precise, since it distinguishes the experiential contemporaneity of that generation (those who were children at the time of the horror) from the pure legacy received by those who were born during or after the development of those events. It is worth clarifying that I myself belong to this generational group (generation 1.5), a fact which obviously affects the arguments I develop in this book.
18 For an analysis of Alejandro Agresti's film work, see Lior Zylberman, "Narrative Strategies of a Post-Dictatorial Cinema. El genocidio en la producción cinematográfica argentina (1984-2007)," thesis presented for the Master's Degree in Communication and Culture, Faculty of Social Sciences, Universidad Buenos Aires, and defended on May 30, 2011.

References

Abraham, N., & Torok, M. (2005). *La corteza y el núcleo*. Amorrortu.
Aspiazu, D., Basualdo, E., & Khavisse, M. (2003). *El nuevo poder económico en la Argentina de los años 80*. Siglo.
Bauman, Z. (2001). *Community: Seeking safety in an insecure world*. Polity Press.
Bignone, R. B. (2000). *El último de facto II. Quince años después*. Centro de Copiado San Miguel.
Bowlby, J. (1973). *Attachment and loss* (3 vols.). Basic Books.
CINTRAS (2009). Daño transgeneracional en descendientes de sobrevivientes de tortura. In CINTRAS, EATIP, GTNM/RJ and SERSOC, *Daño transgeneracional. Consecuencias de la represión política en el Cono Sur*. European Union-Gráfica LOM
Crenzel, E. (2011). El estigma sobre la militancia todavía tiene vigencia. In *Página/12*, July 31th, p. 18.

Drucaroff, E. (2011). *Los prisioneros de la torre. Política, relatos y jóvenes en la postdictadura*. Emecé.
Duhalde, E. L. (1999). *El Estado terrorista argentino. Quince años después, una mirada crítica*. Eudeba (first version appeared in 1984).
Edelman, G. M., & Tononi, G. (2000). *A universe of consciousness: How matter becomes imagination*. Basic Books.
Faimberg, H. (1996). El telescopaje (encaje) de las generaciones (acerca de la genealogía de ciertas identificaciones). In Kaës, R., Faimberg, H. et al. (Eds.), *Transmisión de la vida psíquica entre generaciones*. Amorrortu.
Feierstein, D. (1997). *Cinco estudios sobre genocidio*. Acervo Cultural.
Feierstein, D. (2000). *Seis estudios sobre genocidio. Análisis de las relaciones sociales: Otredad, exclusion, exterminio*. EUDEBA.
Feierstein, D. (2005). *Genocidio. La administración de la muerte en la modernidad*. Eduntref.
Feierstein, D. (2009). El peligro del redireccionamiento de los conceptos del derecho Internacional: Las Naciones Unidas, la Corte Penal Internacional y el nuevo papel de los EE.UU. In *Revista de Estudios sobre Genocidio*. EDUNTREF (vol. 3, pp. 83–97).
Feierstein, D. (2012). The concept of genocide and the partial destruction of the National Group. *Logos. A Journal of Modern Society & Culture*, *11*(1). https://logosjournal.com/2012/winter_feierstein/
Feierstein, D. (2014). *Genocide as social practice. Reorganizing society under Nazism and Argentina´s military juntas*. Rutgers University Press. (Spanish original version: *El genocidio como práctica social: entre el nazismo y la experiencia argentina*, Buenos Aires, FCE, 2007.)
Feierstein, D. (2015a). *Juicios. Sobre la elaboración del genocidio II*. FCE.
Feierstein, D. (2015b). Debates on the criminology of genocide: Genocide as a technology for destroying identities. *State Crime Journal*, *4*(2), 115–127.
Feierstein, D. (2018). *Los dos demonios (recargados)*. Marea.
Feierstein, D. (2019). Human rights? What a good idea! From universal jurisdiction to crime prevention. *Genocide Studies and Prevention: An International Journal*, *13*(3), 9–20. https://doi.org/10.5038/1911-9933.13.3.1669. https://digitalcommons.usf.edu/gsp/vol13/iss3/4
Gatti, G. (2008). *El detenido-desaparecido. Narrativas posibles para una catástrofe de la identidad*. Trilce.
Izaguirre, I. et al (2009). *Lucha de clases, guerra civil y genocidio en la Argentina, 1973-1983. Antecedentes. Desarrollo. Complicidades*. Eudeba.
Jaspers, K. (1946). *Die Schuldfrage*. Lambert Schneider.
Klein, N. (2010). *La doctrina del shock. El auge del capitalismo del desastre*. Paidós.
Mántaras, M. (2005). *Genocidio en Argentina*. Chilavert.
Marín, J. C. (1996) [1979]. *Los hechos armados. Argentina, 1973-1976. La acumulación primitiva del genocidio*, Buenos Aires, pi.ca.so./La Rosa Blindada.
Novaro, M., & Palermo, V. (2003). La dictadura militar 1976/1983. *Del golpe de estado a la restauración democrática*. Paidós.
O'Donnell, G. (1997). *Contrapuntos. Ensayos escogidos sobre autoritarismo y democratización*. Paidós.
Romero, L. A. (1994). *Breve historia contemporánea de la Argentina*. Fondo de Cultura Económica.

Suleiman, S. R. (2008). *Crises of memory and the second world war*. Harvard University Press.
Terranova, J. (2004). *El ignorante*. Tantalia/Crawl.
Tulving, E. (1972). Episodic and semantic memory. In E. Tulving, & W. Donaldson (Eds.), *Organization of memory* (pp. 381–403). Academic Press.
Vezzetti, H. (2002). *Pasado y presente. Guerra, dictadura y sociedad en la Argentina*. Siglo XXI.
Wemmers, J. A. (2021). *Compensating Crime Victims, Report prepared for the Office of the Federal Ombudsman for Victims of Crime*. Government of Canada. March 2021. https://www.victimsfirst.gc.ca/res/cor/CCV-CCV/index.html#_Toc75174997
Yofre, J. B. (2006). *Nadie Fue*. Edivern.
Yofre, J. B. (2007). *Fuimos todos*. Sudamericana.

5
THE SYMBOLIC ENACTMENT OF GENOCIDE THROUGH REPRESENTATIONS IN THE SURVIVOR SOCIETY

In 2000, I wrote a study on genocide in Spanish in which I introduced the concept of "symbolic enactment of genocidal social practices."[1] This concept was further explored in my 2007/2014 publication, "Genocide as a Social Practice" (Feierstein, 2014). However, I want to clarify that this concept has occasionally been misunderstood. When a concept is open for discussion, it can take on a life of its own. Therefore, I want to use this chapter to explain how I define "symbolic enactment" and how it relates to the way in which genocidal processes are remembered and represented in society.

Genocidal social practices are not just carried out through the physical destruction of certain groups or subgroups that are perceived as a threat. They are also enacted in the symbolic and ideological realm, through the representation and narration of the traumatic experience. That is what we have seen through all of this first volume of the trilogy, analyzing the different levels in which these narrations work (neurological, psychological, historical, sociological, transgenerational).

Just as the sale of a product is necessary to "realize" the value it has generated in the production process, the symbolic representation of the destruction of certain groups through genocidal practices is necessary to fully "realize" these practices and generate their intended effects. If the genocidal practices fail to be "represented" through symbols and some kind of representation and narrations connected with them, the destruction of social relations remains incomplete.

In a commercial operation, goods must be sold at a profit to keep the business running. In the same way, genocidal practices need to produce symbolic representations to keep the genocide running. Otherwise, it will result in incomplete destruction of social relations and an inability to accomplish

DOI: 10.4324/9781003336464-6

the desired outcome in the social fabric. To succeed in the long run, the destruction of social relations requires symbolic representations, and symbolic representations take the form of narrations of the past connected with the present and the current identities.

In the case of genocidal social practices, a process occurs similar to what happens in the exchange of commodities and the production of value. The material destruction of certain groups, which takes place in the field of *production* through methods such as concentration camps, and the spread of terror, must also be carried out in the field of *symbolic representation* through certain ways of narrating and representing the experience of destruction.

The goal of this book has been to analyze the purpose of genocide in terms of social relations. Simply eliminating the bodies that represent these relations is not enough to achieve genocidal goals. It is also important to change the social relations that these bodies represented. For genocide to succeed, it must prevent either a return to previous models of social relations or the creation of similar ones in the future. This may also involve transforming the social territory in which these relations take place.

Not all forms of representation effectively obscure or destroy the social relations that genocidal practices aim to eliminate. Not all representations of genocidal acts result in their "symbolic enactment." Just as a product may fail to "realize" its surplus value, a genocide may also fail to be "realized." This failure will occur if terror does not produce highly specific forms of social representation that effectively change the social practices of the survivors.

Not all forms of representation, then, allow for the creation of new models of social relations and not all of them are able to do it in the same way. Not all forms of memory or forgetting serve this purpose and, again, even if some of them could be useful anyone would do it in its own way. Many official "rememberers," for example, perform ceremonies in the naive belief that they can exorcise the specter of genocide merely by invoking its name. We are constantly being "forbidden to forget." Contrary to what these good people may think, however, *total oblivion* is not the most dangerous symbolic enactment that genocide can produce. The disappearance of certain forms of social cooperation does not mean they cannot reappear at a later date. In this sense, *total oblivion* would be a half-hearted symbolic enactment, a "dumping" of the material production of annihilation that would not prove effective in the long run.

Applying Foucault's approach to the functioning of power (Foucault, 2001 [1975]), we need to focus less on what genocidal social practices aim to destroy (a particular culture or political tendency) and more what they aim to achieve (usually a specific way of reconfiguring social relations between people). This includes the ways in which the original, productive genocide must be remembered or reinterpreted.

It is important, then, to examine the ways in which post-genocidal societies tend to narrate the facts of extermination in a way that disconnects genocide from the social order that produced it, not through the crude and obvious denial of the facts, but by altering the meaning, logic and intentionality attributed to them. To achieve greater conceptual precision, let us now consider three fundamental questions:

1 Who is responsible for this final stage of genocide?
2 What forms do symbolic enactments take?
3 How stable are they?

The perpetrator of a genocide is not directly responsible for its symbolic enactment

Placing symbolic enactment on a timeline of genocide is an important step to viewing genocide as a social practice. It means accepting that genocide has effects extending beyond the extermination and that these depend on specific ways of representing the extermination in the surviving society.

However, this may lead to confusion about who is *responsible* for this final stage. The perpetrator may not control all stages of a genocide. For example, stigmatization or harassment may have occurred before the perpetrator came to power, and in some cases may have been present in a society for generations. Nevertheless, the perpetrator is at least primarily responsible for the most visible and legally identifiable moments of a genocide, namely isolation, systematic weakening and annihilation of population groups (Feierstein, 2014).

On the other hand, the perpetrator of genocidal practices does not have the ability to directly influence the ways in which the surviving society will process the terror. In fact, many perpetrators are also affected by the practices they experience, and their own memories and representations are also a result of the effects of this terror (in this case, the terror they have caused, rather than the terror they have suffered, which nonetheless has lasting effects). The effects of terror on the perpetrator who commits heinous acts (kidnapping, torture, rape, murder, concealing evidence) have received little research, but these are also essential for a complete understanding of any genocide.

Therefore, the perpetrators cannot be the direct agents of the symbolic enactment of a genocide. At most, they can act as *indirect agents* if they have the explicit intention of using the consequences of terror for this purpose. There are historical examples that demonstrate this intention, although it is not always the case. In this second role, some of the planners of a genocide may *expect terror to generate certain effects*, without being able to produce themselves more than the terror itself. Their capacity for *indirect action* in relation to the consequences of terror, often explicit, can be traced in numerous documents, the most explicit of which is, for the Argentine case, the Army's *Psychological Operations Regulations*, drafted in November 1968. There it is stated, among other numerous affirmations:

> The method of compulsive action [...] will act on the instinct of self-preservation and other basic tendencies of man (the unconscious) [...] appealing almost always to the fear factor. The psychological pressure will engender anguish; the massive and generalized anguish will be able to derive in terror and that is enough to have the public (target) at the mercy of any subsequent influence.
> *(Argentine Army, 1968, pp. 14–15)*

Nevertheless, this document also states that

> The method of compulsive action will be used exceptionally because of the limitations imposed by ethical reasons and because of the dangerousness of its effects, *which may lead to counterproductive responses.*
> *(Argentine Army, 1968, pp. 15–16)*

These extracts from the Argentine Army's (1968) manual on psychological warfare show that the military understood the profound psychological effects of using terror against civilian targets ("the public"). However, it warns that the effects of such terror may be *unpredictable*. It follows, then, that the perpetrators of a nation-wide genocide could not have hoped to shape the processes of memory or understanding of terror (conscious or unconscious) that emerged after the terror had taken place.

What the manual does state, however, is that *widespread fear and anxiety* can weaken people's sense of self and make them more susceptible to having their identity changed. This effect, produced by the horror of murder, torture and rape, has been confirmed by many genocide survivors (Feierstein, 2014). Now, it is notable that there is a recurrent pattern in the representation of the genocidal past: *only when the voice of the perpetrator confirms it can the voice of the survivor be heard.* This gives us insight into the role that post-genocidal societies assign to each of them.

However, Raphael Lemkin, the creator of the concept of genocide, had already identified the function of terror as a means of destroying the national identity of the oppressed and imposing the national identity of the oppressor (Irvin-Erickson, 2017; Lemkin, 1944). This is why we have also focused on symbolic enactment and its effects on the transformation and reorganization of identity structures, as well as what Ricœur refers to as *narrative identities* (Ricœur, 1984–1988, 2004).

The use of torture, murder, rape, mistreatment and humiliation can cause severe damage to a person's identity, but it is not a guaranteed method of controlling how they will form their identity afterward. Though these tactics may be seen as necessary steps in the process of genocide, it is important to understand that the way in which memories and representation function is complex and affected by many variables, and it should not be thought of as a simple or predictable process as we have seen through this whole volume.

The symbols and practices used to deny the victims' identity, shift responsibility and create an abstract representation of horror that is typically associated with a genocide, are not created by the perpetrators. Rather, they are adaptive responses of *the victims, their families and society as a whole* as a result of the systematic and widespread use of terror. In any process of recovery and healing, it is important to address these elements, but it is also important to recognize that the representations of the events must come from the victims and their communities, rather than being imposed by the perpetrators. This is an important point to consider in the process of coping and healing.

Symbolic enactment involves a complex process of constructing memories and representations that does not result in binary resolutions such as "performs genocide" versus "does not perform genocide" or "works through" versus "does not work through"

Another potential misunderstanding when using the concept of "symbolic enactment" is the tendency to classify different ways of remembering the past as either "enacting" genocide or "confronting" and "working through" genocide. This can lead to the belief that only certain representations of the past are acceptable to the victims while others must be seen as belonging to "the enemy."

It is my hope that this work will help to clarify this misunderstanding by highlighting the complexity of memory and representation processes instead of a binary and simplistic view of that process. It is important to note that just because certain narratives have an impact on the healing process, it does not mean they can be easily labeled as politically correct or incorrect. The use of memory and the incorporation of the past into the present is a complex and multifaceted process. It could be also applied to the current debate on the different representations of gender and cultural issues.

In short, the inclusion of symbolic enactment as a part of the genocidal process adds complexity to the analysis, highlighting that the goal of genocide is not just physical destruction, but also the destruction of identity. Identifying the ways in which genocidal practices are symbolically enacted challenges our own memories and forces us to examine the many ways in which terror is perpetuated. This approach requires constant self-reflection and examination of dominant, entrenched ways of constructing memories.

Rather than determining that certain memories are "true" or "healthy," and others are not, this approach encourages self-criticism, examination and understanding of different representation and different perspectives of the past.

The processes of symbolic enactment are not static, but rather contain the dynamism of reality within themselves

Just as it is important to avoid binary thinking in the processes of symbolic enactment, it is also important to understand that memory and representation processes are dynamic and not static. Representations that aid in coping and healing at one point in time may not necessarily play the same role later on. The same memory processes that facilitate coping and healing in one context may hinder these in another context or even within the same community at a different point in time. This has happened with the concepts of human rights, state terrorism or crimes against humanity, as discussed in Chapter 4 of this work, but it could also happen with the concept of genocide and war. In Chapter 4, we also saw that genocide is not immune to future reinterpretations or misuses beyond the interesting ways in which Argentine society deal with it in their different narrations produced during the past 40 years. Indeed, some interpretations not only trivialize it but even legitimize it.

Therefore, the analysis of the processes of symbolic enactment of genocidal social practices must be considered in the context of the specific historical and social conditions in which they occur, and the dominant power dynamics in each context, both locally and internationally. For example, attention must be paid to the competing geopolitical meanings of perpetrator trials and the legitimization of United Nations or United States attacks on Iraq, Afghanistan or Libya. These attacks have led to significant civilian deaths in the name of defending human rights, which highlights the need for a nuanced and context-specific understanding of such issues (Feierstein, 2019).

In Chapter 4, we examined different accounts of Argentina's history. However, these narratives are specific to particular time periods: the final years of the dictatorship (1981 and 1982), until 2022, including the process of reopening trials that began in 2005 and it is ongoing.

It has been noted that in Guatemala, the concept of genocide has often been used to obscure the political motivations behind mass killings and to depoliticize the case as it was not the case in Argentina due the binary and racial interpretation of the genocide concept regarding Guatemala. This that has not occurred in Argentina, despite some attempts to equate the two situations. In contrast, the limited use of the concept of politicide in Argentina, which emphasizes the political nature of violence, has led to a narrow focus on the fight against guerrillas. This in turn has resulted in a view of the conflict as a battle between "two demons," obscuring the broader role of terror as part of the process of "national reorganization."

It is clear, then, that analysis and discussion cannot take place *in a vacuum*. Not only do different concepts and narratives have different implications, discussions about memory must also consider the specificities of a given context. The relationship between concepts, narratives and the movements that create them, as well as local and international power dynamics, must be carefully examined, taking into account how these elements change over time. The concept of symbolic enactment allows us to look beyond the killing itself and investigate the long-term effects of using terror as a tool for social reorganization. This is the central focus of my previous work and the trilogy of which this volume is a part.

Note

1 In 1997, I published *Cinco estudios sobre genocidio* (1997), in which I outlined a periodization of five genocidal processes. However, as I began to view genocide as a social practice whose ultimate goal was the reorganization of social relations, I realized that this practice did not end with extermination but also involved a process of representation and incorporation of terror in the development of the practice. This led me to include a sixth study in a later work (Feierstein, 2000 and again in Feierstein, 2020), specifically focused on the symbolic realization of genocidal social practices.

References

Argentine Army. (1968). RC5-I and RC5-II: *Reglamento de Operaciones Sicológicas*. Instituto Geográfico Militar. https://www.mpf.gob.ar/plan-condor/files/2018/12/5.pdf

Feierstein, D. (1997). *Cinco estudios sobre genocidio*. Acervo Cultural.

Feierstein, D. (2000). *Seis estudios sobre genocidio. Análisis de las relaciones sociales: otredad, exclusion, exterminio*. EUDEBA.

Feierstein, D. (2014). *Genocide as social practice. Reorganizing society under Nazism and Argentina´s military juntas*. Rutgers University Press. (Spanish original version: *El genocidio como práctica social: entre el nazismo y la experiencia argentina*, Buenos Aires, FCE, 2007)

Feierstein, D. (2019). Human rights? What a good idea! From universal jurisdiction to crime prevention. *Genocide Studies and Prevention: An International Journal, 13*(3), 9–20. https://doi.org/10.5038/1911-9933.13.3.1669. https://digitalcommons.usf.edu/gsp/vol13/iss3/4 https://digitalcommons.usf.edu/gsp/vol13/iss3/4

Feierstein, D. (2020). *Nuevos estudios sobre genocidio*. Heredad.

Foucault, M. (2001) [1975]. Truth and juridical forms. In James D. Faubion (Ed.), *Essential works of Foucault, 1954-1984: Power*. Penguin.

Irvin-Erickson, D. (2017). *Raphael Lemkin and the concept of genocide*. University of Pennsylvania Press.

Lemkin, R. (1944). *Axis rule in occupied Europe: Laws of occupation - analysis of government - proposals for redress*. Carnegie Endowment for International Peace.

Ricœur, P. (1984–1988) *Time and narrative* (Kathleen McLaughlin & David Pellauer, Trans.). University of Chicago Press.

Ricœur, P. (2004). *Memory, history, forgetting* (Kathleen Blamey & David Pellauer, Trans.). University of Chicago Press.

INDEX

Note: Page numbers followed by "n" refer to notes.

Abraham, N. 48
accommodation 25, 68, 69
"action-reaction" model 113
activators 19
affect 19–21
affected person 102
Agresti, A. 116, 120, 123n18
AI *see* artificial intelligence (AI)
Alfonsín, R. 59n7, 94, 95
Algeria 93
alienating identification 115
alienation 4, 52, 105, 114–121
Anderson, P. 73
angoisse 19
anosognosia 30
Ansermet, F. 26
anticathexis 40
anti-stimulus protection 52
anxiety, chronic 19
Aplysia 17
Argentina 5–6, 17, 19, 88; Argentine Human Rights Commission (CADHU) 122n6; Association of Former Disappeared Detainees 95; CADHU (Comisión Argentina de Derechos Humanos, Argentine Commission on Human Rights) 95; discourse of war 92–95; genocide in 90, 95–97; Grandmothers of Plaza de Mayo 95, 100; HIJOS ("Children for Identity and Justice Against Forgetting and Silence") 95–96, 116; "Informe Nunca Más" (CONADEP report) 102; military dictatorship (1976–1983) 1; Mothers of Plaza de Mayo 95; National Commission on the Disappearance of Persons (CONADEP) 94, 99+; national reorganization process 89–90; National Security Doctrine 97; "*Never Again*" (CONADEP report) 99; *Nunca Más Report* 94–95; Permanent Assembly for Human Rights 95; *Psychological Operations Regulations* (Argentine Army) 129; remembered present 100–121; Spanish Catholic Church 100; state terrorism in 97–100; state violence and trauma in 5; Trial of the Military Juntas (1985) 94
Argentine Team for Psychosocial Work and Research (EATIP) 3, 49
Aristotle 31
armed conflict 100
artificial intelligence (AI) 13
asomatognosia 30

assimilation 25, 27, 42, 68, 69, 84
Assmann, A. 67
Assmann, J. 62, 67
attention 21, 26
autobiographical memory 12

Bangladesh: genocide in 88
Barcesat, E. 95
Bartlett, Sir F. C. 22, 25, 62, 67–70, 74, 76, 89; *Remembering* 67
Bartsch, D. 20
Bauman, Z. 103
behavioral disorders 38
behavioral inhibition 18–19
behaviorism 17, 54
Benjamin, W. 4, 62, 83, 84; *Theses on the Philosophy of History* 71; Thesis VI 71; Thesis XVII 72, 82; Thesis XIX 72–73
Berezin, A. 54, 55
Bergson, H. 15, 53, 62–66, 72, 88; *Creative Evolution* 63; *Matter and Memory* 29, 62, 63; perception of absence 68; theory of memory processes 65
Bignone, R. B. 106
binocular fusion 30
bonding memory 67
Bowlby, J.: *Attachment and Loss* 59n4, 123n16; "Attachment and Loss" trilogy 34n7
brain: as adaptive organ 12–16; definition of 24; structure 24
Brown, W. 46
Browning, C. 73

Cambodia: genocide in 88
Carri, A. 120; *Los rubios* 116, 119
Cartesian dualism 13
Caruth, C. 47
case histories 83
cathexis 40
causality 106–107; defensive 106
Centro de Salud Mental y Derechos Humanos de Chile (CINTRAS) 114–115
Changeux, J. P. 3, 11, 34n4, 67; *Good, the True, and the Beautiful: A Neuronal Approach, The* 34n4; *Physiology of Truth. Neuroscience and Human Knowledge, The* 34n4
chronic anxiety 19

CINTRAS *see* Centro de Salud Mental y Derechos Humanos de Chile (CINTRAS)
civil war 7, 91, 93, 97, 100, 102, 106, 121n3
classical conditioning 16, 17, 19
Cold War 33n1, 110, 115
collective memory 6, 65, 74, 78, 89, 97, 108
collective trauma 46, 50
Colombia: armed conflict 100
communicative memory 67
conscious: apparatus 34n5; memory 32, 39; representation 28, 40; repression 45; system 15, 26, 31, 37, 38, 48
consciousness 2, 13, 15, 21–22, 27, 28, 31, 32, 45, 51, 62–65, 89; access to 39–42, 48; awareness *versus* 34n5; of being conscious 29; definition of 34n5; language and 28, 64; and "reentrant" processes 22–26; as "remembered present" 25–26; of a superior order 28, 29
Convention on the Prevention and Punishment of the Crime of Genocide 95, 98, 104
"counter-revolutionary" policy 95
creation 32
crimes against humanity 4, 5, 7, 87, 88, 90–92, 96, 99–101, 103, 104, 109, 110, 113, 121n3, 122n10, 131
criminal law 1, 109
critical discourse analysis 88
cross-fertilization 2
crypt 114, 115, 120
cultural memory 67
cybernetics 13

Darwin, C. 13, 15, 22, 24
defensive causality 106
degeneracy 24, 30
degeneration 24
denegative pacts/pact of denial 4, 38, 45, 51–54, 112
Descartes, R.: on mind–body distinction 2
desensitization 4, 15, 17–19, 30, 33, 34n7, 39, 51–53, 57, 58, 90, 112, 121
desubjectivation 121

developmental selection 22
"dictatorship–democracy" divide 111, 115
Diner, D. 73
dirty war 92–94, 112, 121–122n5
dreams 32
Drucaroff, E. 116–117, 119, 123n17
Duhalde, E. L. 95, 97–99, 121n2, 122n6
Durkheim, É. 65
dynamic nucleus hypothesis 26–28

EATIP *see* Argentine Team for Psychosocial Work and Research (EATIP)
Edelman, G. 3, 4, 11–13, 30, 33–34n2, 41, 62, 63, 67, 70, 76, 89; *Bright Air, Brilliant Fire* 34n2; on development of consciousness 22–23; dynamic nucleus hypothesis 26–28; Neural Darwinism 13, 15, 21–22, 25, 31, 33n2, 34n6, 41; *Neural Darwinism* 34n2; *Remembered Present, The* 64n2; *Second Nature. Brain Science and Human Knowledge* 34n2; *Universe of Consciousness. How Matter Becomes Imagination, The* 34n2; *Wider than the Sky. The Phenomenal Gift of Consciousness* 34n2
ego 38
Ejército Revolucionario del Pueblo (Revolutionary People's Army) 92
episodic memory 28, 88–89
epistemology 41; psychogenetic 25
equilibration 25, 44, 66, 68, 69
escraches 117–118
Etchecolatz, M. O. 7
ethnicity 5
evolutionary theory 13, 15
experiential selection 22
external stimuli 43, 44

Faimberg, H. 115
Falklands-Malvinas War (1982) 106
Feierstein, D. 122n11; *Cinco estudios sobre genocidio* 132n1; *Genocide as Social Practice* 1; *Seis estudios sobre Genocidio (Six Studies on Genocide)* 1

Ferenczi, S. 46
fidelity–truth distinction 71
"fight or flight" response 16, 19, 21
fMRI *see* functional magnetic resonance imaging (fMRI)
Fonagy, P. 37
forced disappearance 90
Ford Foundation 122n8, 123n15
Former Yugoslavia: genocide in 88
Foucault, M. 127
French counterinsurgency doctrine 93, 122n5
Freud, S. 2–3, 13, 14, 26–28, 31–32, 34, 76, 88; *Beyond the Pleasure Principle* 2, 31, 39, 45; on conscious apparatus 34n5; *Inhibitions, Symptoms and Anxiety* 39, 51, 53; *Interpretation of Dreams, The* 39; *Moses and Monotheism* 2; *Mourning and Melancholia* 123n16; on nature of the unconscious 37; *Project for a Scientific Psychology for Neurologists and Psychologists* 44, 62–63; *Psychology for Neurologists* 2, 28; on repetition compulsion 21, 27, 38, 43, 45, 50, 51, 53, 64, 83, 89, 112; on repression 39–45; theory of drives 43; *Totem and Taboo* 2; *Unconscious, The* 39–40; on working-through (*Durcharbeiten*) 37, 49, 53–56, 64, 83; *Works on Metapsychology* 39; *see also* individual entries
Friedländer, S.: *Probing the Limits of Representation. Nazism and the "Final Solution"* 73
functional magnetic resonance imaging (fMRI) 10
Funes the Memorious 20
Funkenstein, A. 73

García Reinoso, G. 54, 55; *Psychogenesis and the History of Science* 3; *Sistemas Complejos (Complex Systems)* 3
Gatti, G. 119–120, 123n17
gene expression/regulation 20
generational battle cry 118
generational telescoping 115

genocide 1, 5–7, 122n6; in Argentina 95–97; depoliticized 98; perpetrator of 128–130; Rwandan 85n3, 88; symbolic enactment of 4, 57, 65, 126–132; *see also individual entries*
Ginzburg, C. 73
Gramsci, A. 93
Guatemala 5
Guinzburg, C. 75

habituation 16–18
Halbwachs, M. 62, 65, 67, 70, 78, 89; *Social Frameworks of Memory, The* 66
healing 5–7, 59n6, 79, 87, 95, 100, 101, 105, 111–114, 130, 131
historical discourse analysis 71
history: as a field beyond memory 73–81; and memory, old debate between 70–73; meta-history 79; question of methodology or procedures 77–79; question of objectives 76–77; question of sources 74–76; representation, forms of 79–81
homicide 90
human cognition 12, 13
human engineering 54
human rights 123n15; abuses 88, 121n5, 122n6, 122n8, 122n10; organizations 6, 95, 98, 103, 111, 113, 122n8; violations 6, 91, 103, 109, 111
hypercathexis 40–41
hysteria 27, 45, 50

id 38, 40
identity 87–123; memory and 4; narrative 62, 81–85, 129
image-memories 63, 65
image-remembrance 29
impunity laws 6, 117
independent memories 63
individual autonomy 103
Indochina 93
inferential processes 68
instinctual impulses 43–44
intelligence 64; artificial 13
inter-American Human Rights Conventions 109
International Criminal Court 109
International Tribunals 109

irreversibility 122n13
Isaurralde, H. 7
Izaguirre, I.: *Lucha de clases, guerra civil y genocidio en la Argentina, 1973–1983. Antecedents. Development. Complicidades* 121n3

Jaspers, K. 123n14
Jean, I. S. 34n8
Joffre 122n14

Käes, R. 3, 4, 37–38, 48–49, 51
Kandel, E. 3, 11, 16, 17, 19, 20, 24, 26, 27, 32, 34n3, 41, 62, 67
Kirchner, C. F. de 122n6
Kirchner, N. 122n6
Klein, N. 122n8; *The Shock Doctrine. The Rise of Disaster Capitalism* 33n1

Laborit, H. 18–19
LaCapra, D. 50, 53, 58, 73, 76, 77
Lang, B. 73
language and consciousness, relationship between 28, 64
Laplanche, J.: *Dictionary of Psychoanalysis* 46
Lashley, K. 10
Latin America: National Security Doctrine 88
Lehrer, J. 11
Lemkin, R. 129
Levinas, E. 15, 82
Leys, R. 47
Libya 104, 109
literary criticism 46
long-term emotional memories 41
long-term memory 15, 16, 23, 26, 27; construction of 19–21
Lorenzo, N. 7

Magistretti, P. 26
Mántaras, M. 96
Marín, J. C. 93, 121n3
masochism 43
Meijide, F. 95
melancholia 30
memory: and action, relationship between 4, 28, 62–65, 111; autobiographical 12; bonding 67; collective 6, 65, 74, 78, 89, 97, 108;

communicative 67; conscious 32, 39; consolidation, theory of 63; construction of meaning 28–33; cultural 67; disorders 2; episodic 28, 88–89; and history, old debate between 70–73; and identity 4; imprint 31; ineffable 4; irrational 4; long-term 15, 16, 19–21, 23, 26, 27; non-representational model of 31; physical location of 32; as a process 88–91; processes 10–34; recall 21; as representational inscription 31; responses 16–18; semantic 28, 88; and sensory perception 28; short-term 15, 16, 19, 20, 23; social frameworks of 65–67, 78; transmission experiments 67–70; traumatic 16, 27, 46–48
mental apparatus 38, 39, 46, 48, 50, 52
meta-history 79
mind–body distinction 2, 12
mnemonic imprint 31
Montoneros 92
Moscovitch, M. 63
Moses, D. 82
Müller, G. E. 63
Myanmar: genocide in 88

narrative identity 62, 81–85, 129; definition of 81
national group 104–105
natural selectionism 13
Nazism 97, 98, 108
neoliberalism 122n8
Neural Darwinism 13, 15, 21–22, 25, 31, 33n2, 34n6, 41
neural plasticity 11, 25, 69
neuronal communication 14, 23; dynamic nucleus of 23
neuroscience 1–4, 10–34, 38, 42, 46, 47, 62, 63, 65, 66, 70, 71, 87, 88
Nietzsche, F. 27
non-meaning, ideologies of 4
nonsense, ideology of 52–53, 56, 57
Novaro, M. 113, 122n5, 122n9
Nuremberg trials 74

objective historiography 71, 72
obsessions 38
Ogawa, S. 10

ontology 15
oppression 72, 89, 107, 129
oral histories 74
over-remembering (hyperthymesia) 20

Palermo, V. 113, 122n5, 122n9
pantheon 114
partial destruction of the national group 108
Pavlov, I. 17
phobia 21, 27, 38, 45, 50
phrenology 32
physical location of memory 32
physiological stimuli 43
Piaget, J. 13, 25, 76; *Equilibration of Cognitive Structures, The* 3; *Psychogenesis and the History of Science* 3; theory of equilibration 68, 69
Pilzecker, A. 63
plasticity: of brain functioning 13; neural 11, 25, 69; synaptic 17
political group 104–105
Pollak, M. 74
Pontalis, J. B.: *Dictionary of Psychoanalysis* 46
popular struggle 95
post-traumatic stress disorder (PTSD) 46, 59n5
power relations 56
preconscious system 38, 40, 42
Prince, M. 46
psychic apparatus 2, 18, 28
psychic imprint 49
psychic structure 33
psychoanalysis 1–3, 12, 13, 15, 28, 37–39, 43, 54, 58, 59n6, 62, 63, 65, 66, 70, 71, 83, 87
psychogenetic epistemology 25
PTSD *see* post-traumatic stress disorder (PTSD)
Puget, J. 3, 4
punishment 17, 87

question: of analogies 107–110; of methodology or procedures 77–79; of objectives 76–77; of sources 74–76

Ranke, L. von 71, 72
rape 90
reconciliation 117
reductionism 12

"reentrant" processes: consciousness and 22–26; reentrant signaling 22–24
refusal to accept responsibility 118
relations of transference 77
remembered present 100–121; causality 106–107; consequences 110–111; effects on form of appropriation and alienation 114–121; effects on generational transmission 114–121; effects on possibility of mourning 114–121; healing and prevention 111–114; question of analogies 107–110; victims, definition of 101–105
repetition 19–21, 51–53; compulsion 21, 27, 38, 43, 45, 50, 51, 53, 64, 83, 89, 112
representation: forms of 79–81, 88; symbolic 127
repression 21, 27, 33, 37, 39–41, 51–53, 55, 57, 59n6, 83, 93, 96, 107, 123n15; conscious 45; origin of mechanism of 43–45; primary 45; primordial 50; secondary 45; state 103, 113
repressors 20
resilience 54, 55
revolutionary war 102, 106, 108, 112
Reyes Mate, M. 72, 82–83
Ricœur, P. 3, 62, 71, 79–81, 129; *Memory, History, Forgetting* 79; on narrative identity 81–85; *Time and Narrative* 79, 81
Romero, L. A. 96, 99
Rose, H. 10
Rose, R. 10
Rose, S. 14
Rosenfield, I. 3, 11, 32
Rozanski, C. 7
Rwandan genocide 85n3, 88

Sábato, E. 102
Sacks, O. 11
sadism 43
Sargant, W. 46
scene 29
Schmitt, F. 10
School of the Americas 93
Scilingo, A. 122
Seineldín, M. A. 116
selection 24; developmental 22; experiential 22

selective synapse stabilization 34n4
self-constancy 82
self-sameness 82
semantic memory 28, 88
sensitization 16–17, 19
sensory-motor systems 25
short-term memory 15, 16, 19, 20, 23
Social Darwinism 15
social frameworks of memory 65–67, 78
social sciences 78
social trauma 48, 50
Spencer, H. 15
Squire, L. R. 18
Sri Lanka: genocide in 88
state: repression 103, 113; terrorism 4, 5, 7, 88, 91, 96–101, 103, 106, 107, 109, 111, 113–116, 118, 121n2, 121n3, 131; violence 4, 5, 12, 48–49, 52, 73, 90, 105, 108, 109, 112
Strachey, J. 2; *Standard Edition of the Complete Psychological Works of Sigmund Freud, The* 43
subjectivity analysis 71
sublimation 43, 54
substitutive formation 45
superego 38, 49
survival of the fittest 15
symbolic enactment of genocide 4, 57, 65, 126–132
symbolization 14, 25, 38, 48, 50
synaptic plasticity 17

Terranova, J. 116, 120; "El ignorante" 118, 119
terrorism: state 4, 5, 7, 88, 91, 96–101, 103, 106, 107, 109, 111, 113–116, 118, 121n2, 121n3, 131
terrorist state 95, 97–99, 103, 109, 121n2
theory of the two demons 94, 113
thing-presentation (presentation of the thing) 59n1, 59n2
thing-representation 39–42, 48
Tononi, G. 11, 89; *Universe of Consciousness. How Matter Becomes Imagination, The* 34n2
Torok, M. 48
torture 48, 56, 57, 90, 91, 96, 98–102, 128, 129
totalitarianism 103

"totalizing" approach to human suffering 47
transference analysis 71
trauma 37; collective 46, 50; definition of 46; historical 48; social 48, 50; social processes of recovery from 54; *see also* traumatic
traumatic 45–50; definition of 45, 46; event 4, 31, 32, 46, 47, 51, 52, 72, 76, 83, 87, 120, 123n17; memory 16, 27, 46–48; pasts 71; *see also* trauma
"Trieb" (motivational drive) 43, 59n3
"Trieblehre" (theory of motivational drives) 43
truth–fidelity distinction 71

unconscious 4, 26–28, 34n5, 37–45, 47, 48, 51, 53, 57, 64, 69, 75, 76, 78, 79, 89, 99, 115, 117, 129; attraction 45; mind 21, 39, 112; representation 40, 41; system 15, 26, 31, 37–41, 50
United States 93
urgency 20

Van Der Kolk, B. 46–47
variation 22
Vezzetti, H. 113, 122n9
victims 112; definition of 101–105; direct 101, 105; indirect 101; secondary 101; tertiary 101

Viñar, M. 57, 58
violence 113, 114; self-criticism of 118; state 4, 5, 12, 48–49, 52, 73, 90, 105, 108, 109, 112

Walsh, R.: Open Letter to the Military Junta 96
war: civil 7, 91, 93, 97, 100, 102, 106, 121n3; Cold War 33n1, 110, 115; crimes 87, 93, 94; dirty 92–94, 112, 121–122n5; discourse of 92–95; generational impact of 115; revolutionary 102, 106, 108, 112; theories of 94–95
warfare 93, 100, 129
war on terror 109
White, H. 73, 79–81
Winocur, G. 63
word-presentation (presentation of the word) 59n1
word-representation 39–42, 48, 50, 57, 64
working-through (*Durcharbeiten*) 37, 49, 53–56, 64, 83, 130–131; definition of 53; as social and historical process 56–58

Zeman, A. 13, 34n5

Printed in the United States
by Baker & Taylor Publisher Services